"Lee McIntyre has emerged as our foremost scholar of science denial and an intellectual activist combating the attempted assassination of truth. In the teeth of fake news, alternative facts, conspiracy theories, identity politics, postmodernism, and epistemological relativism, McIntyre's *On Disinformation* expertly identifies who the enemies of truth are and how to counter their claims with reason, science, and compassion. A tour de force of scholarship and advocacy." —Michael Shermer, Publisher, *Skeptic* magazine; Presidential Fellow, Chapman University; author of *Conspiracy*, *The Believing Brain*, and *Why People Believe Weird Things*

"McIntyre's latest book connects the sordid history of science denial and climate denial to today's election denial, exposing how interests exploit disinformation and work fissures in our society to weaken citizens' trust in our democracy and in one another." —Sheldon Whitehouse, US Senator, Rhode Island

"In post-truth America, reality isn't dying by accident or suicide; it's being poisoned on purpose. Lee McIntyre—a philosopher of knowledge as well as a student of disinformation—names the culprits and exposes their methods. Even more important, he shows how to foil the crime. *On Disinformation* is the brisk, bracing primer that everyone should read on how to make America truthful again." —Jonathan Rauch, Senior Fellow, Brookings Institution; author of *The Constitution of Knowledge: A Defense of Truth*

ON DISINFORMATION

ON DISINFORMATION

HOW TO FIGHT FOR TRUTH AND PROTECT DEMOCRACY

LEE MCINTYRE

The MIT Press
Cambridge, Massachusetts
London, England

The MIT Press would like to thank the anonymous peer
reviewers who provided comments on drafts of this book.
The generous work of academic experts is essential for
establishing the authority and quality of our publications.
We acknowledge with gratitude the contributions of these
otherwise uncredited readers.

This book was set in Arnhem Pro by New Best-set
Typesetters Ltd. Printed and bound in the United States
of America.

Library of Congress Cataloging-in-Publication Data

Names: McIntyre, Lee C., author.
Title: On disinformation : how to fight for truth and
    protect democracy / Lee McIntyre.
Description: Cambridge, Massachusetts : The MIT Press,
    [2023] | Includes bibliographical references and index.
Identifiers: LCCN 2022042939 (print) | LCCN 2022042940
    (ebook) | ISBN 9780262546300 (paperback) |
    ISBN 9780262375597 (epub) | ISBN 9780262375580 (pdf)
Subjects: LCSH: Disinformation—Political aspects—
    United States. | Denialism—Political aspects—United
    States. | Communication in politics—United States. |
    United States—Politics and government—1989-
Classification: LCC JA85.2.U6 M45 2023 (print) |
    LCC JA85.2.U6 (ebook) | DDC 320.97301/4—dc23/
    eng/20230315
LC record available at https://lccn.loc.gov/2022042939
LC ebook record available at https://lccn.loc.gov/2022042940

10 9 8 7 6 5 4 3 2 1

For Dave Corkran,

who lit the spark . . .

CONTENTS

CONTENTS

1
TRUTH KILLERS

The storming of the US Capitol on January 6, 2021, was an American tragedy. It was also completely predictable. The "patriots" in face paint—who carried sharpened flagpoles, bats, and zip ties into the Senate chamber—were the inevitable result of seventy years of lies about tobacco, evolution, global warming, and vaccines. After the "truth killers" provided a blueprint for how to deny scientific facts that clashed with their financial or ideological interests, it was a small step for unscrupulous politicians to figure out how to use this strategy to lie about anything they wanted, such as the baseless claim that the 2020 presidential election was stolen and that the January 6 insurrectionists were actually "peaceful protestors" or Antifa in disguise.

Welcome to the world of reality denial, where truth is subordinate to ideology, feelings have more weight than evidence, and democracy hangs in the balance. Throughout history, autocratic leaders and their wannabes have understood that the quickest way to control a population is to control their information sources. But in a society that still has a free press, disinformation is the new censorship. Remember that scene in *Indiana Jones and the Last Crusade* where Harrison Ford has finally found the Holy Grail but can't tell which one it is because it's surrounded by a hundred fakes? That's the point of disinformation. If you can't hide or destroy the truth, surround it with bull-shit. You can always kill it later.

The post-truth playbook goes like this: attack the truth tellers, lie about anything and everything, manufacture disinformation, encourage distrust and polarization, create confusion and cynicism, then claim that the truth is available only from the leader himself. The goal is not merely to get people to believe any particular false claim, but to so demoralize them with a tsunami of falsehoods that they begin to give up on the idea that truth can be known at all, outside a political context.

In her landmark work on totalitarianism in the twentieth century, political philosopher and Holocaust historian Hannah Arendt said it best: "The ideal subject of totalitarian rule is not the convinced Nazi or the convinced communist, but people for whom the distinction[s] between fact and fiction . . . true and false . . . no longer exist."[1] More recently another Holocaust historian, Timothy Snyder, put it even more succinctly: "post-truth is pre-fascism."[2]

We've got less than a year to figure this out. Now that Kevin McCarthy and the Republican faithful have succeeded in retaking the House in the 2022 midterm elections—which means that the GOP was effectively rewarded for having embraced Trump's "big lie" in 2021—they're perfectly positioned to install Trump (or whomever they like) as president, no matter the vote count in 2024. After that, some wonder how close we'll be to Orwell's nightmare: $2 + 2 = 5$ in the basement of the Ministry of Love.

Once truth dies, the end may come swiftly for American democracy. Like Russia and China, we'll still have politicians in suits going about a charade of the people's business in the halls of government, we may even have further elections, but it won't really matter. If the truth killers succeed in using reality denial to undermine democracy, the next day we'll wake up in an electoral dictatorship.

2
THE HISTORY OF STRATEGIC DENIALISM

Denialism is not a mistake—it's a lie. It is crucial to distinguish between ordinary misconceptions and targeted manipulation—between *mis*information and *dis*information. Those in the media, government, education, and the rest of us have got to stop thinking of our current epistemic crisis as if it were some sort of accident or natural disaster. It is instead a coordinated campaign being run by nameable individuals and organizations whose goal is to spread disinformation out to the masses—in order to foment doubt, division, and distrust—and create an army of deniers.

The truth isn't dying—it's being killed.

People do not wake up one day and spontaneously wonder if the California wildfires were caused by a Jewish space laser or if the COVID-19 vaccines might contain microchips. Those are instead the result of a propaganda campaign that was deliberately engineered to raise doubt where there was none, because it served the interests of the people who invented it. These sorts of interests can be economic, political, or ideological, but the point is that denialism is intended to benefit the people who *create* the lies, not the people who believe them.

Modern science denial began on December 15, 1953, when the heads of four of the largest US tobacco companies gathered at the Plaza Hotel in New York City, along with a public relations specialist to advise them on what to do about a forthcoming scientific study that drew a link between cigarette smoking and lung cancer. His advice? Fight the science. Take out full-page ads in American newspapers. Hire your own scientists to create an alternative narrative. Reach out to newspaper and magazine journalists, editors, and publishers to get them to tell "both sides" of the smoking controversy. Lean heavily on the idea that this is an open scientific debate where nothing has yet been "proven." The goal: to get the public to question the truth about something that scientists didn't really question.

And it worked.

By 1955, a public opinion poll on tobacco use indicated that "neither the press nor the public seems to be reacting with any noticeable fear or alarm."[1] The tobacco companies rode that wave of doubt for the next forty years as they continued to profit, right up through a 1994 congressional hearing, when the new heads of the seven largest tobacco companies testified that they did not think nicotine was addictive. By that point a lot of people didn't believe them, but the industry's goal had been fulfilled. Their job all those years hadn't been to prove that smoking did *not* cause lung cancer, but to raise enough doubt about whether it did to delay things while they sold more cigarettes. In 1998, "big tobacco" was finally busted and hit with the largest civil fine in US history—$200 billion—after which they were allowed to continue selling cigarettes (with new restrictions on advertising) with the understanding that the cat was now out of the bag, because everyone knew that smoking was dangerous. Years later, in 2004, a leaked 1969 memo surfaced which proved that industry executives had known all along that their product was deadly.

In their insightful book *Merchants of Doubt*, Naomi Oreskes and Erik Conway provide rich detail on this "origin story" of modern US science denial and contend that it created a blueprint that was later used by others to deny the truth about acid rain, the ozone hole, and—most notoriously—global warming. In many works since, scholars and journalists have shown that fossil fuel companies followed the "tobacco strategy" to the letter and created their own decades-long campaign of obfuscation and delay—including sponsorship of "contrarian" scientific work, donations to members of Congress, funding for annual conferences hosted by "think tanks" to raise doubt about whether there was a scientific consensus on climate change, and a public relations campaign meant to soften their image—all while they continued to profit. It later came out, through a series of their own leaked memos, that the fossil fuel companies had known the truth about global warming as far back as 1977.[2]

One naturally thinks of all this as a crime against the good-faith effort of scientists to bring the facts before the US public, so that policy makers can heed their warnings in time to do something to save people's lives. But, from the point of view of those with special interests that conflict with the empirical findings of science, this had all been a ringing success. And this success surely came to the attention of those who sought to extend the reach of strategic denialism to topics far beyond science.

One imagines some ambitious, orange-haired politician making the cynical leap of inference from cigarettes and global warming to other fact-based beliefs: "Why, if they can get away with lying about *that*, I can lie about anything at all."

And he did.

The truth killers now had a new target: not just science, but reality itself.

3
THE CREATORS

MAGA is not just a political movement—it's a good old-fashioned denialist campaign. Fifteen years ago, cognitive scientists discovered that all science deniers follow the same flawed reasoning strategy:[1]

(1) cherry-pick evidence
(2) believe in conspiracy theories
(3) engage in illogical reasoning
(4) rely on fake experts (and denigrate real experts)
(5) have impossible expectations for what the other side must achieve

This explains why (1) climate deniers like Ted Cruz always seem to highlight the same (and later corrected)[2] scintilla of data that once suggested there hadn't been a rise in global temperature between 1997 and 2015, while ignoring all of the voluminous data since then—drawn from surface air temperature, sea ice loss, extreme weather events, and even the larger context of the satellite data that Cruz was citing—which formed the basis for Reuters's 2019 statement that the evidence in favor of anthropogenic climate change was now so strong that it was a million-to-one shot that the climate deniers could be right.[3] It also explains why (2) Flat Earthers believe that the true shape of the Earth is being withheld by all government leaders, astronauts, pilots, and scientists, who are in league with the devil, or why anti-vaxxers contend that the CDC paid off the

Institute of Medicine to suppress the data that allegedly prove that the MMR vaccine causes autism. Why (3) anti-maskers believe that re-breathing into an N95 mask can *give* you COVID-19. Or (4) that hydroxychloroquine or ivermectin is a better response to COVID-19 than the Pfizer and Moderna vaccines. And then there is always the old chestnut whereby (5) antievolutionists, climate deniers, and all the rest contend that scientists need to *prove* their results, or else their own denialist beliefs are just as credible.

In an earlier book, *How to Talk to a Science Denier*, I explore such folly in detail in search of a way to engage science deniers about the content of not just their false beliefs but also the corrupt pattern of logic leading up to them. But the problem today is that this same toxic form of reasoning has now metastasized from science denial to *reality* denial—from claims that evil researchers are putting microchips into our vaccines, to claims that nefarious state election officials somehow rigged the 2020 presidential election and then destroyed all the evidence.

By the end of his presidency, the *Washington Post* reported that Trump had lied over 30,000 times during his four years in office.[4] But none of Trump's lies were more virulent, or more dangerous for democracy, than his big lie about the 2020 election (and the violent insurrection it sparked), which fulfills each of the five tropes of denialist reasoning:

(1) Cherry-picking: Even after the highly partisan "fraudit" review of ballots in Maricopa Country, Arizona, had concluded that *Biden* won the election, Trump and his allies

continued to cherry-pick statistics from the final report, suggesting that long-debunked claims hadn't yet been investigated.[5]

(2) Conspiracy theories: As part of the Arizona audit, officials were at one point searching for "bamboo fibers" in the ballots themselves, based on a Trumpian conspiracy theory that 40,000 ballots had been flown in from East Asia and stuffed into ballot boxes.[6] Other debunked conspiracy claims involved "rigged" voting machines, suitcases of "lost" ballots, magic Sharpie markers, and even one involving Italian military satellites that were alleged to have erased Trump votes.[7]

(3) Illogical reasoning: Immediately after the January 6 insurrection, Trump and his allies maintained that no actual violence had occurred and that his followers were merely "peaceful protestors." At the same

time, they began to spread the rumor that any violence must have been due to Antifa or other "false flag" operatives in disguise.[8] But how could both claims be true?

(4) Fake experts: Trump's team used an organization called "Cyber Ninjas" to conduct the Arizona audit, even though they had no previous auditing experience and no expertise in elections.[9]

(5) Impossible standards: Despite exhaustive evidence and debunking by experts, Trump and the majority of his followers refuse to give up their false belief that the 2020 election was stolen, until it is *proven* that it was *not* stolen.[10]

Ask yourself whether #StopTheSteal fits this five-step pattern and you have your answer as to whether it qualifies as a full-fledged denialist campaign. But this audacious lie didn't spring up by itself. As with all forms of denialism, there is a purposeful path that leads down the rabbit hole, and it starts with disinformation.

Here is just a sample from Trump's rally speech to his supporters on January 6, 2021.

All of us here today do not want to see our election victory stolen by emboldened radical-left Democrats, which is what they're doing. And stolen by the fake news media. That's what they've done and what they're doing. We will never give up, we will never concede. It doesn't happen. You don't concede when there's theft involved.

Our country has had enough. We will not take it anymore and that's what this is all about. And to use a favorite term that all of you people really came up with: We will stop the steal. Today I will lay out just some of the evidence proving that we won this election and we won it by a landslide. This was not a close election.[11]

Three things are necessary for strategic denialism to be successful. Disinformation must be created, it must be amplified, and it must be believed. If one's objective is merely to delay the truth long enough to reach some short-term goal (say, to make a profit), it is probably sufficient merely to raise doubt. But if one's objective is not to delay the truth but to kill it—if one's long-term goal is political or ideological—it is necessary to foment distrust.

Denialist beliefs often elicit an incredulous response by those who do not share them, for they cannot understand how—even in the face of overwhelming refutatory evidence—a denier will refuse to give them up. Why does this happen? Because denialist beliefs are not based on facts in the first place; they are rooted in identity. Hundreds of experiments have been performed by social psychologists over the last seventy years that demonstrate the social nature of belief. From Solomon Asch's classic 1955 experiment (which showed that 33 percent of subjects would misreport which line was longer, if others in their group had already done so) to more contemporary experiments involving moral misjudgments (which show that we will give a "moral excuse" to someone who does something wrong, if they are wearing the same randomly assigned colored wristband that we are wearing),[12] the evidence for conformity and even "tribalism" in belief is rock solid.

Even empirical beliefs are heavily influenced by community, trust, values, and how we see ourselves in relation to the people around us. Indeed, there is probably good evolutionary reason for this.[13] Who is more likely to get their genes into the next generation? The iconoclast who keeps insisting that they are right (even if they are) or the one who gets along better with others? Truth is only part of the equation. But this opens the door to manipulation, based on a full-blown propaganda campaign or a smooth-talking liar sitting around the campfire.

The goal of disinformation is not just to get you to question some particular fact about a piece of reality that clashes with the disinformer's interests, but to erode your trust in the "truth tellers" on the other side. This undercuts the basis for a whole class of factual beliefs all at once. The genius of disinformation is that it doesn't just get you to believe a falsehood, but to distrust (and sometimes even hate) anyone who does not also believe this same falsehood. That is why a strategic denialist campaign like the one against climate change became so much more effective once it was politicized, because then it could exploit partisan enmity and not just doubt. And the same thing is true, of course, with vaccine denial, election denial, and Trump's entire #StopTheSteal campaign. To get someone to trust only the information sources that *you* provide them—and distrust any other information sources as biased or misleading—is the disinformer's dream.

Don't just lie, polarize. Create a news silo. Exploit any preexisting grievance and resentment. Make it "us against them." The other side is not just biased, they are lying to you. These are evil people. Perhaps they even deserve to be physically assaulted or thrown in jail. In this environment, one can sell an alternative narrative of reality even when there is no evidence to support it, and a mountain of refuting evidence to suggest it's not true. As long as the narrative appeals to the emotions of what your team *wants* to believe—and they have been conditioned to think that it is what a loyal team member is *supposed* to think—you can get them to assert the truth of almost anything. This is why distrust, and not just doubt, is the prime objective of a denialist campaign. Mere doubt can be overcome with evidence, but distrust cannot.

Does this sound familiar? It should. It is the tobacco strategy on steroids.

In my 2018 book *Post-Truth*, I defined this notion as the "political subordination of reality" and argued that science denial is one of its precursors. That there is a straight line between the manufacture of doubt about whether cigarettes cause lung cancer and today's conspiracy-fueled dumpster fire of disbelief about any facts that conflict with one's political agenda. This is no longer just about science, but reality itself. And it is no longer motivated solely by money, but ideology and power. What began with a few tobacco executives at the Plaza Hotel culminated seventy years later on the steps of the US Capitol. Denialism has now become a political litmus test for the Republican Party. And its highest expression is MAGA.

Trump's call to arms on January 6 was unsuccessful, in that it did not result in overturning a free and fair election; the insurrectionists were not able to get their hands on Mike Pence or Nancy Pelosi, and there was no coup. Yet in another sense, #StopTheSteal has been a ringing success . . . and it is far from over.

Sixty-six percent of Republican voters still think the 2020 election was stolen, and that Trump is the rightful president.[14]

A stunning 147 Republican members of Congress still refuse to publicly acknowledge that Joe Biden is the legitimately elected president of the United States.[15]

Why do they believe these things?

Because Donald Trump wants them to.

#StopTheSteal is not merely an attempt to overturn the last election—it is a propagandistic effort meant to undermine voters' confidence that there *is* such a thing as a fair election, so that Trump can steal the next one. Indeed, isn't that what the "fraudit" in Arizona was really about?[16]

Trump's embrace of disinformation as a political weapon began even before he was president. What began with "birtherism" and claims that Hillary Clinton was going to cheat in the 2016 election sailed straight through the early days of Trump's presidency, when he lied about whether he had lost the popular vote, the size of his inauguration crowd, and even whether it had rained during his inauguration speech.

In the following months, as Trump's propaganda campaign settled over the United States, it achieved its intended purpose. We were confused and disoriented. Few understood what had hit us. Why was Trump lying so much? Had the man no shame? Some of the lies were even about things that were easily refuted by evidence. But why, then, did so many people seem to believe him? Trump was dismissed as a fool by many, but he had mastered something no one else had ever succeeded in: the application of Russian-inspired disinformation tactics to US politics.[17]

Modern disinformation warfare was invented in the 1920s, courtesy of Feliks Dzerzhinsky, founder of Vladimir Lenin's Cheka, which evolved into a succession of three-letter Russian intelligence agencies such as the GPU, the KGB, and today's FSB, SVR, and GRU. In his book *Active Measures*, Thomas Rid tells the story of disinformation as a political weapon and traces its evolution from Lenin's successful campaign to wage psychological warfare against the enemies of the Russian Revolution, right up through today's Internet Research Agency, which expanded Russia's counterintelligence toolkit through the dark arts of hacking, phishing, digital leaks, and the amplification of carefully fabricated lies from government-sponsored troll farms. Within the GRU, there are special units devoted to psychological warfare (unit 54777), cyber and hacking operations (unit 26165), and the strategic release of politically sensitive information (unit 74455). Russia's current president Vladimir Putin—formerly a KGB officer in East Germany—is well known for using the tactics of information warfare not only against foreign enemies but against his own citizens as well. As such, Putin provided a model for how reality denial could be extended to domestic politics.

How did Trump become aware of this and conceive the goal of emulating Putin? Many forget that Trump had a lot of business dealings in post-Soviet Russia, so he had a chance to study its society up close. With the assistance of unscrupulous advisors such as Steve Bannon and Roger Stone, it is easy to imagine the appeal of a strategy that allowed one to advance one's own interests through the creation of an alternative narrative of reality.[18] As Bannon so memorably put it, "The Democrats don't matter. The real opposition is the media. And the way to deal with them is to flood the zone with shit."[19] Even if the truth tellers found the holy grail, would anyone recognize it?

Two of the most common tactics that Trump borrowed from Putin's disinformation-fueled leadership style are the "firehose of lies" and "whataboutism." The firehose of lies is when someone advances a series of multiple and contradictory explanations, usually in response to criticism of a situation that makes them look bad.[20] According to Kiril Avramov, an expert from the University of Texas on Soviet and Russian disinformation tactics, this is disorienting and intended to disrupt the use of logic to find truth. A prime example is when Putin responded to the poisoning of Sergei Skripal in Britain in 2018,[21] by saying it was the fault of Britain, "and/or Ukraine. And/or it was an accident. And/or it was suicide. And/or it was a revenge killing by relatives. And/or Russia did not produce the nerve agent that was used."[22]

The tactic of whataboutism is another Putin favorite, where—when your opponent begins to make too much sense—you change the subject to something unrelated, such as when an American reporter challenged Putin in Geneva in 2021, pointing out that "the list of your political opponents who are dead, in prison, or jailed is long. . . . What are you so afraid of?" Putin responded by bringing up the January 6 insurrection, offering that "many countries are going through exactly what we're going through . . . we sympathize with what was happening in the States, but we do not wish that to happen in Russia."[23]

Both techniques are truth killers and fit right into the political subordination of reality. The narrative you present is the one you would prefer to be true; in its support you employ an array of disinformation tactics—including the exploitation of cognitive bias through mere repetition—which may be enough to make your version of the truth sound credible. But the overall goal is not simply to persuade but to so confuse and disorient your opponent that they become cynical and break into different camps over how to respond. As Avramov recently put it, "the more fragmentation and atomization the better you can manipulate a population. This goes back to totalitarian measures and techniques for population control. You don't have to be a KGB or Stasi officer to know this."[24]

Trump has used these truth-killing techniques—and a plethora of others borrowed from Russian intelligence—throughout his MAGA campaign.[25] Look for instance at the ridiculous (and contradictory) assertion that the January 6 insurrectionists were just "peaceful protestors" or "ordinary citizens," alongside claims that this was a false flag operation, where the people in attendance were not actually Trump supporters but troublemakers from the Black Lives Matter (BLM) movement or Antifa in disguise. But how could both be true? Trump later used this same technique to great effect when he responded to the FBI's discovery of classified documents at Mar-a-Lago by saying that the FBI had "planted" them, but also that he had declassified them all before he left the White House. The firehose of lies is alive and well. Trump's use of whataboutism is also quite obvious, such as when Trump was challenged in a Fox News interview by host Bill

O'Reilly, who said, "Putin is a killer," and Trump responded, "There are a lot of killers. You got a lot of killers. What, you think our country is so innocent?"[26] The idea here is to create a sort of false equivalence, which undermines the idea that it is possible to offer an objective answer to any factual question. If all truth is narrative, then one narrative is just as good as another, right? And if the truth is unknowable, then what is the point of pursuing blame and accountability?

With all of this Russian influence, one might naturally wonder whether Russia might be responsible not just for inspiring Trump's strategy but also for some of the content behind MAGA. If so, it wouldn't be the first time Russia has infiltrated an American denialist campaign. Questions linger over whether Russia was responsible for creating and amplifying some of the disinformation that helped Trump win the 2016 election, but without access to the unredacted Mueller Report it is hard to have a definitive answer. What is not in doubt, however, is that for the past two decades, Russia has been actively involved in a disinformation campaign that fuels some of the most virulent forms of American science denial. On a range of topics from vaccines (both before and since COVID-19), HIV/AIDS, Ebola, 5G, GMOs, climate change, and beyond, Russia has for years been pumping out propaganda meant to undermine Americans' trust in science.[27] As one expert put it, Putin's goal is to target "the institutions we rely on to understand the truth."[28]

Since the onset of the coronavirus pandemic, this has ramped up considerably into a "vaccine war" between Russia and the West, which Putin views as a successor to the 1957

Sputnik space launch—a matter of Russian pride. It was in Putin's interest to show that the Pfizer and Moderna vaccines are dangerous, in order to advance his narrative that the Russian vaccine "Sputnik V" is exemplary, and to encourage its use throughout the world. This was accomplished through disinformation.[29]

Evidence for this was first reported in the *Wall Street Journal*, which explained that Russian intelligence had been deliberately creating and pushing anti-Western vaccine stories through four of its English-language propaganda arms.[30] In April 2020, for instance, the *Oriental Review* published a story claiming that any forthcoming Western vaccines were likely to contain biometric microchips, courtesy of Bill Gates, who had allegedly taken out patent number 060606 on this technology.[31] Near the bottom of the article were buttons to make it easier for readers to share this story on Face-book and Twitter, which they did. Only a month later, CBS News reported on a poll that found that 44 percent of Republicans thought that the microchip story was true.[32] (Note that this was a full seven months before the first COVID-19 shots were available to the general public, and nearly five months before the Pfizer and Moderna vaccines had even been developed.) Ironically, the Russian propagandists did such a good job that it apparently backfired, causing some vaccine hesitancy in Russia as well.[33]

Putin is certainly a truth killer in his own right (if we had any doubts about that, his virulent disinformation campaign during the war on Ukraine can leave no doubt), but does this mean he was behind #StopTheSteal or the January 6 insurrection? Surely Russia has an interest in creating chaos and unbalancing the United

States, and would cheer on and perhaps exploit any campaign to undermine our interests. After all, while we are preoccupied with our own internal divisions, it is harder to spare any bandwidth for problems coming out of Russia. But that does not mean Russia is responsible for all of the disinformation and denial that has come out of MAGA world.

A much more plausible answer for who is responsible for America's recent slippage into reality-denying crazy town is staring us right in the face: it's Trump. Trump may have learned from Putin, but he is a world-class truth killer in his own right.[34] While it is easy to dismiss Trump as a buffoon, Jonathan Rauch has argued that he is actually a "genius-level propaganda operative."[35] And whether Russia was behind some of the content (or amplification) of MAGA disinformation, or just created the blueprint, it took someone to put it all into practice—and that was Trump himself.[36]

In doing so, Trump has created his own model of chaos and deceit for other truth killers to follow. After Trump lost the 2020 election, he made an enormous effort to rally his base and use it to threaten any Republican politicians who did not show sufficient fealty to him and his outrageous lie about the 2020 election. Indeed, one of the most amazing things about Trump's disinformation campaign is that he has used it not only against millions of US voters but hundreds if not thousands of government officials as well. Even as the twice-impeached, single-term, biggest loser in the modern history of US politics,[37] Trump still controls the agenda of the Republican Party and has managed to convince a majority of them that the best way to win a future election is not to appeal to voters but to change the election laws (and gum up the works of the January 6 investigation), so that maybe next time he won't need an insurrection to cement his grasp on power.

Following the 2020 election, lawmakers in nineteen states passed thinly disguised voter suppression laws, designed to make voting more difficult for the Democratic Party's base.[38] More ominously, in some states they changed the laws to empower legislatures to substitute in their own slate of electors, if they feel that there are adequate grounds to question an electoral outcome. In the 2022 midterm elections, 291 election deniers ran for office at the state and federal level. While a majority of big-name candidates like Kari Lake and Doug Mastriano lost in the governor, secretary of state, and attorney general races in swing states like Arizona, Michigan, Nevada, Pennsylvania, and Wisconsin—which prevents a good deal of mischief at the state level in certifying the 2024 presidential election—what got lost in celebration was the fact that 179 of those 291 deniers won their races, including 175 in the US House, which represents an increase in the 139 Republicans who voted against the electoral college count immediately following the January 6 assault on the US Capitol.[39] The fact that over sixty courts have dismissed Trump's claims of election fraud and irregularities as meritless does not seem to matter to these sorts of true believers. Trump's big lie is the gift that keeps on giving, not just for Trump but for all Republicans, for it serves as justification for a power grab that could portend the end of American democracy.

It is shocking to watch just how easily so many Republican officials have been co-opted into doing Trump's bidding. Whether they are following Trump out of agreement or simple self-interest, it doesn't really matter. They are following him. Even though Trump is now out of office, his propaganda campaign has been picked up by the entire GOP establishment, who seem to believe that it is in their best interests to continue Trump's war on truth. Like the tobacco and fossil fuel executives before them, they too have become truth killers.

And somewhere that ultimate truth killer Vladimir Putin must be smiling. In a 2021 article in *Foreign Affairs* entitled "The Kremlin's Strange Victory," Fiona Hill argues that this would be the ultimate triumph for Russia.[40] Not just when we leave them alone, but when we become just like them.

4
THE AMPLIFIERS

Without a means of amplifying a propagandist's message, disinformation is useless. Yet just a little amplification can have a devastating impact. According to a 2021 study put out by the Center for Countering Digital Hate, 65 percent of the anti-vax propaganda on Twitter was due to just twelve people.[1] In an internal study, Facebook found that 111 of their accounts were spreading half of all the anti-vaccine disinformation on their site.[2] These small numbers demonstrate how much damage can be done by just a few highly motivated people, and the incredible reach of disinformation when a liar has a megaphone.

Indeed, sometimes the number of people responsible for deciding to spread bad information can be counted on one hand. Think of Rupert Murdoch and his vast media empire, which has arguably toppled two world governments and played a prime role in destabilizing American democracy.[3] The "Fox News Effect" was discovered in 2012, when academic researchers at Fairleigh Dickinson University found that regular viewers of Fox's highly partisan, selectively biased "news" coverage *were less well informed than if they had watched no news at all.*[4] Worse, many feel that Fox News is responsible for the tremendous polarization that has gripped the US electorate over the last several years, by creating a news silo that few of its viewers ever break out of. In a 2020 Pew

Research study, it was found that 65 percent of Republicans named Fox News as their most trusted news site; in comparison to Democrats, they also named vastly fewer other news sites that they trusted at all.[5]

None of this would be so bad if the information that Fox News chose to broadcast were simply partisan. Unfortunately, there is growing evidence that, especially in recent years, Fox has begun to report stories that come straight out of Russian-government funded news sources such as RT (Russia Today), which are little more than state-controlled propaganda.

In his book *Hoax*, journalist Brian Stelter tells the story of how a 2016 Russian-manufactured conspiracy theory—regarding the murder of Democratic National Committee (DNC) staffer Seth Rich—found its way onto the popular morning show *Fox and Friends* because (as a Fox News employee later revealed in a lawsuit) it "advanced President Trump's agenda."[6] This is not to mention Sean Hannity and other Fox hosts' extensive coverage of WikiLeaks during the 2016 presidential campaign, which is now known to have been the result of a Russian influence operation.[7] Or the more recent shilling that Tucker Carlson—Fox's most popular media host—has been doing for Vladimir Putin's propaganda efforts in support of his war against Ukraine.[8] Alarmingly, Carlson's program is sometimes rebroadcast to an appreciative Russian audience on Kremlin state-sponsored television.[9]

The amplification of disinformation can be incredibly damaging, especially when one is hearing only one side of the story. Add to this the shadowy world of dark money that has contributed to all of the lobbying, films, rallies, and other events to promote Trump's big lie—including even the January 6 insurrection itself—and one understands the crucial role that just a few individuals can play in the amplification of disinformation.[10] In her 2021 article "The Big Money behind the Big Lie," Jane Mayer provides the evidence to conclude that a tide of money—mostly funneled through conservative interest groups such as the Bradley Foundation, Turning Point USA, True the Vote, the Heritage Foundation, the Federalist Society, and others—are doing for election denial what the tobacco and fossil fuel industries did for science denial.[11] She traces the origin and spending of millions of dollars that have funded dozens of antidemocratic "election integrity" projects (and also litigation), the support of conservative anti-vote candidates, and the Arizona recount itself. Mayer quotes

US Senator Sheldon Whitehouse, who says, "It's a massive covert operation run by a small group of billionaire elites. These are powerful interests with practically unlimited resources who have moved on to manipulating that most precious of American gifts—the vote."

But the mainstream media should not be let off the hook either. Even if they may not knowingly create or amplify disinformation, traditional news outlets do sometimes unnecessarily hype stories by cherry-picking the most sensational parts of them—in order to drive a narrative of conflict, failure, and chaos—which exacerbates polarization and increases audience engagement. In a 2022 essay in the *Washington Post*, columnist Jennifer Rubin writes:

> We are all too familiar with the journalistic inclination to make every story into

a political sporting context denuded of moral content or policy substance. *Who does this help? How did Biden fail? Aren't the Republicans clever?* This sort of framing is unserious and unenlightening, failing to serve the cause of democracy, which is under assault around the globe.[12]

Even if they are not in the same league as thinly disguised partisan propaganda outlets like Fox News, OANN, and Newsmax, major news outlets like CNN and MSNBC have their own interests that are sometimes orthogonal to telling the truth. In an interview for the documentary film *Broken Media*, Chris Hayes—one of the prime-time anchors on MSNBC—admitted that even the most well-intentioned networks and journalists inevitably butt up against the problem of "confirmation bias":

Every media outlet constructs narratives. . . . The problem is when you subvert the complexity and the facts to the dominant story you're telling. That's a real danger and it happens all the time—when relevant facts are left out because they don't fit the narrative thrust of the story you're trying to tell.[13]

Hayes goes on to say that this type of bias seems wired into the human brain, because we all have a "tribal instinct towards finding information we like and disregarding information we don't like." But the problem comes when news networks use this as an excuse to target their coverage toward the known biases of their audience, sometimes blurring the distinction between fact versus opinion programming. One may try to defend MSNBC with the claim that they "aren't as bad as Fox"—because they engage *only* in confirmation bias and aren't making up facts—but such easy acceptance of the inevitability of bias plays right into the hands of the propagandist, whose goal is to convince us that truth is impossible because everyone is biased. This, of course, falls far short of the courtroom standard to "tell the truth, the whole truth, and nothing but the truth." But it also falls short of what journalistic ethics should require.

The foremost imperative of a news outlet should be to tell the truth. At times, of course, this ideal conflicts with an individual reporter's desire not to be accused of political favoritism. If the truth falls mostly on one side of the partisan divide, might this not suggest to a polarized audience that the person who reports it is not being objective? One handy solution is to indulge the reflex to "tell both sides of the story."

Yet in an environment rife with disinformation, this is the worst possible way to report on a factual matter, because it not only gives oxygen to a lie but might tacitly suggest that the truth lies somewhere in between. Neither objectivity nor neutrality require one to feign indifference between the truth and a lie; to refuse to stand up for the truth because it might look partisan is itself to succumb to partisanship.

Fortunately, this point is occasionally made by journalism professors who shape the next generation of reporters. In one scalding example attributed to Jonathan Foster, a lecturer in journalism at the University of Sheffield, one student remembers him saying: "If someone says it's raining and another person says it's dry, it's not your job to quote them both. Your job is to look out of the fucking window and find out which is true."[14]

It is imperative that journalists seek a higher standard of reporting than the false dichotomy between political bias on the one hand and massaging a story in order to avoid the *perception* of bias on the other. One must eschew false equivalence, deplatform liars, report disinformation within the context of a "truth sandwich," and in general learn to take more seriously the problem of "information bias" (where an audience is less well informed than when they started), which can be even more dangerous than political bias.[15] Even if left-leaning networks such as MSNBC are not as bad as Fox News, it is not particularly respectful of truth to tell only the part of the story that feeds one's narrative and misses the larger picture. In CNN and MSNBC's thousands of hours of coverage on Trump's war on truth, for instance, why has there been so little reporting that takes even the small step of tagging what is going on as disinformation rather than misinformation?[16]

As Masha Gessen argues in *Surviving Autocracy*, the media must stop normalizing Republican election denial as if it were merely a political dispute. Journalists should have learned by now to treat both Trump and his apologists as they would a hostile foreign autocratic regime. As Gessen puts it, in describing a 2020 dust-up at the *New York Times* over whether to call Trump a liar: "By choosing to act as though in the war on reality it was possible not to choose sides, the *Times*—and with it, the American media mainstream—became, reluctantly though not unwittingly, the president's accomplices."[17] Julia Ioffe, a Russian American journalist who has published extensively in the *Atlantic*, the *New York Times*, and many other venues, drew the conclusion even more sharply in a 2022 tweet: "the only people who were fully prepared to cover the Trump presidency properly were people who knew how authoritarian regimes worked. The Washington press corps, which treats politics as something between a baseball game and a Broadway show, was woefully unprepared."[18]

Mainstream media can be truth killers too—or at least bystanders who refuse to render aid when the truth is dying. Even now that Trump has left office, his surrogates routinely appear on many of the prestige Sunday morning news shows to amplify his disinformation. Former CNN anchor Soledad O'Brien has excoriated this practice, saying that one of the simplest ways to fight disinformation is not to book liars on your program.[19] Almost as bad, some networks have demonstrated hostility toward truth by promoting a hyped-up narrative of failure and chaos within the Biden administration, in order to serve their own interest of not wanting to appear as if they are somehow aligned with the Democrats. In his important essay "How Media Coverage Drove Biden's Political Plunge," Perry Bacon Jr. has argued that after so many years of (justifiably) negative coverage of Trump, many in the media were desperate to find a big anti-Biden story that might inoculate them against accusations of left-wing bias.[20] And they found it in Biden's somewhat chaotic withdrawal from Afghanistan. This kind of performative objectivity, where journalists search for negativity anywhere they can find it and exaggerate what little they can find, had the truth-twisting effect of making it seem as if Biden's transgressions were somehow equal to Trump's. Even with the January 6 committee hearings providing a steady stream of evidence of Trump's corruption and criminality, the media spent most of the summer of 2022 pounding the story of inflation and high gas prices, which are worldwide problems and cannot credibly be linked to any specific policy failure of the Biden administration. Nonetheless, Biden's poll numbers fell sixteen points since the beginning of his presidency to 39 percent as of July 2022, which is equivalent to Trump's in July 2020, a month when a record 25,000 Americans died of COVID-19 and cases doubled in nineteen states.[21] True objectivity be damned, "bothsidesism" allowed the mainstream media to protect its own reputation for alleged impartiality.

But don't forget that there is another all-important measure of journalistic self-interest: ratings. It is a little-known fact that not just Fox News but also CNN and virtually every other major news network gets their ratings on a minute-by-minute basis.[22] If a story isn't appealing to the audience, that can affect coverage. Even at "objective" news organizations, the importance of a story can sometimes take a back seat to viewer engagement. Polarization and a "horse race" are good for both ratings and profit. I sometimes wonder if executives at all three of the major cable news outlets didn't wish that every year were election year.

And then, of course, there is the role played by social media.

The importance of Facebook, Twitter, and YouTube in spreading misinformation and disinformation on the Internet is not in dispute. As three of the five most visited websites in the world, how could it be otherwise? Yet the issue is not simply how much false information is out there on these sites, but what public harm this has caused and what the companies are doing to stop it.

Despite protests to the contrary, these companies make minimal efforts to police for disinformation, yet love to call attention to what they *have* done, even if it is only minuscule in proportion to the problem. Yes, it was good when YouTube decided in 2020 to crack down on election misinformation on its site, which had a virtuous spillover effect on Facebook and Twitter.[23] And, yes, it was good when Facebook and Twitter both began to get more serious about providing content warnings about both election and coronavirus misinformation in 2020. But this raises the question of why these companies do not do more to combat misinformation and disinformation on other topics all the time.[24] Of course, tech executives can be expected to bristle at this characterization, preferring to highlight the *number* of accounts they have closed and the *number* of messages they have taken down. But this always reminds me a bit of the "greenwashing" advertisements one sees from ExxonMobil and other fossil fuel companies talking about their efforts to research algae and other alternative fuels, even though this accounts for less than 1 percent of their annual research budget.[25] Companies often report the top line number, but where is the denominator?

The truth is that most social media companies do not do a very good job of policing for disinformation, likely because it is not in their financial interest to do so.[26] In 2016, Mark Zuckerberg said it was "crazy" to think that misinformation on Facebook might have helped Trump win the presidential election. By 2017, he admitted that more than 150 million people had viewed Russian propaganda posts before the election.[27] Since then, one grows tired of hearing Facebook brag that it has closed 1.3 billion fake accounts or taken down 18 million misleading posts, without any admission of how many people saw or shared those posts.[28] And how many have they missed? Despite Zuckerberg's 2021 statement that Facebook has spent $13 billion on "safety and security" since 2016—and that it has a human team of 40,000 scrubbing for misinformation—this pales in comparison to the scope of the problem and the potentially horrible consequences for American democracy if they do not get this right.[29]

Could Facebook and other tech companies do more to fight disinformation on their platforms? Of course, if they cared to. How do we know this? Because they already do it for other odious content. Ask yourself this: when was the last time you saw pornography, suicide, beheadings, or other acts of terrorism on Facebook? The answer is likely never. That's because Facebook employs a human team that scrubs for this type of content, so it never makes its way onto our news feeds. It's got to be the worst job at Facebook, but they care enough to pay attention to it, because it would likely hurt their bottom line if they did not.[30] So couldn't they do the same for disinformation? Yes, if they cared enough.

What Facebook does and doesn't care about was revealed in a 2021 *Wall Street Journal* series called "The Facebook Files," which was facilitated by leaked documents from whistleblower and former Facebook employee Frances Haugen.[31] In follow-up congressional testimony, Haugen revealed that Facebook *knows* that it and its affiliates are doing harm—through damaging self-esteem and increasing thoughts of self-harm among teenage girls who use Instagram, and through increased polarization of the electorate from Facebook's relentless algorithmic promotion of sensational content in order to goose "engagement"—but it does little to stop it. In Sheera Frenkel and Cecilia Kang's 2021 book *An Ugly Truth*, they detail how profit-driven decisions by top Facebook executives have facilitated and enabled a cover-up of the company's harms in the interest of making a buck, even at the cost of promoting hate speech, lies, and disinformation.[32]

Now it is important to point out here that—unlike partisan media outlets like Fox, Breitbart, Newsmax, and OANN—social media companies like Facebook, Twitter, and YouTube do not seem to be *intentionally* spreading disinformation. Even after Elon Musk's controversial takeover at Twitter—which resulted in a radical cutback in content moderation—there is no evidence that Twitter is deliberately amplifying disinformation. Even so, whether deliberate or not, their inaction and neglect can cause incredible harm. Even if all the tech companies did was make it easier for their users to share false information, this is bad enough. And of course, some of Facebook's behavior *is* witting . . . or at least little more than willful ignorance, if Haugen's testimony is to be believed. Facebook *knows* that its focus on engagement leads to hatred, polarization, and the potential for violence. That's why it tweaked its algorithm just before the 2020 presidential election, hoping not to repeat the debacle of fake news that spread on its platform in the run-up to the 2016 election. But they then turned the dials back immediately after the 2020 election—and the result was January 6.[33]

Most of the amplification of disinformation that happens on social media is (technically speaking) unwitting—it's literally nonhuman—because it is based on algorithms, which are machine-based learning tools that study our preferences, then respond by giving us more of what we seem to like. If that is videos of dogs who are befriended by ducklings, we'll get more of that; if it's content that maintains the Democratic Party is run by a cabal of pedophiles, we'll get that instead. Although the algorithms used on social media are created by human beings, they work so quickly and relentlessly that in actual practice they can take on a life of their own, which exacerbates the possibility that something might go wrong without anyone realizing until it is too late. In one heartbreaking example from 2017, misinformation and hate speech on Facebook set off a round of suicide bombing and executions in India, which then spilled over into a genocide of the Rohingya people in Myanmar.[34] In response, just prior to a $150 million lawsuit by some Rohingya refugees, Facebook said that it would hire more people with "language, country and topic expertise" in countries like Myanmar.[35]

Clearly, the solution is not merely to play whack-a-mole with misinformation and disinformation as it pops up on Facebook. The larger problem seems to be how to anticipate and stop the algorithmic spread of propaganda on social media before its human scrubbers even know there is a problem. How many engineers at Facebook are working on this? This information has not been made public. The contents of its algorithms are a secret to anyone outside the company.

In a 2021 article on the algorithmic amplification of disinformation on social media, Mathew Ingram writes in *Columbia Journalism Review* that "the algorithms themselves, and the inputs they use to choose what we see in our feeds, are opaque. They're known only to senior engineers within those companies, or to malicious actors who specialize in 'computational propaganda.'"[36] Even if no human being actually intends it, automated algorithms at virtually all the social media companies seem primed to spread false information and incendiary rhetoric because they are formulated to maximize engagement, clicks, and time spent on the site. Rather than promote truth, they are engineered for profit. But knowing this, it is at least disingenuous for tech executives to say that these problems are all entirely unwitting (because they reflect no human intention to mislead), so they should get credit simply for working on the problem. As Zuckerberg once wrote, "if we didn't care about fighting harmful content, then why would we employ so many more people dedicated to this than any other company in our space?"[37] Yet the question remains, are they doing enough? If it is possible for Facebook, Twitter, and YouTube to modify their algorithms in service of promoting more accurate information, yet they choose not to, doesn't that make them at least an accessory to the truth killers' mission?

Some tech insiders have pushed back against this sort of characterization, or even the claim that there is rampant *dis*information on the Internet, by hiding behind the notion that most people who share false stories likely do so because they believe them to be true, which technically makes them *mis*information. But does that really make it any better? The origin is still a lie. When bad actors create and/or publicize a story that they *know* to be false, this is of course deplorable; but when a fool picks up those lies and shares them because it triggers their amygdala—or they choose to be lazy or willfully ignorant—is it really less dangerous?

In a 2021 article entitled "Don't Blame Russian Trolls for America's Anti-Vaxx Problem," Sophie Zhang—a former Facebook employee—claims that the idea of Russian responsibility for disinformation on social media is overblown, because most misinformation is spread by domestic sources.[38] But even if this is true, it misses the point and goes straight to the heart of why big tech's strategy to fight misinformation on its platforms seems doomed to failure. Even if disinformation is spread "authentically" by people who believe it to be true, *the information at issue is still a lie* that was weaponized by the propagandists who created it. When Nicki Minaj spread the bogus claim to her 22 million Twitter followers that COVID-19 vaccination might lead to swollen testicles and perhaps infertility, shouldn't it matter whether these bogus claims might have originated from some disingenuous disinformer?[39] Thus Facebook's efforts to fight misinformation primarily by cracking down on "inauthentic" sharing (which was Zhang's job at Facebook) seems a misfire: disinformation is no less benign because it is shared by useful idiots rather than Russian bots.

Now, if true, perhaps it is a good thing that most of the misinformation on the Internet is shared authentically by actual human beings, because this means that most of the content we would like to crack down on isn't necessarily being amplified by the truth killers themselves. If it were, just imagine the difficulty of solving the problem, for how do you get a creator of disinformation to stop making or spreading it as much as they can? Yet if most is shared by the unwitting, then we have a chance.

Amplification is the key pinch point in the disinformation highway from creation to amplification to belief. Perhaps we can't stop the creators from making disinformation—and once it's believed, it is in some ways too late—but maybe we can put a kink in the supply chain between these two points. If we're going to stop the truth killers, this is likely where we'll do it.

But how?

Flagging content isn't enough. Even removing fake accounts and taking down misleading posts isn't enough either. Social media companies' efforts so far have been woefully inadequate, not because they don't know what to do, but because there has so far been little incentive for them to do it. With no sustained external pressure, most tech companies will likely continue to fail to act in proportion to the seriousness of the problem. To stop the truth killers from succeeding, we must get more serious about fighting the amplification of misinformation and disinformation, and for that we need to create more reason for both partisan and social media outlets to curb the role that they play in propagating polluted content.

How do we do that?

A first step might be to restore the "Fairness Doctrine." From 1949 until 1987, when the Federal Communications Commission (FCC) repealed it, the Fairness Doctrine had dictated that all news outlets that used the public airwaves must give equal time to opposing viewpoints. This forestalled the possibility of completely partisan editorializing and guaranteed at least some balance in broadcasting, probably in part by keeping extremist shows off the air, because the network would then be required to provide time for rebuttal. After the Fairness Doctrine was repealed, one of the most popular radio shows to enjoy its new freedom was Rush Limbaugh in 1988. This opened the floodgates for the first broadcast of Fox News on television in 1996, and all that followed.

One of the driving forces behind repeal of the Fairness Doctrine was the idea that it interfered with freedom of speech. Despite calls to reinstate it—in light of some of the harms that became obvious a few years later—in 2008 even President Obama felt that, instead of this, it was more important to focus on "opening up the airwaves and modern communications to as many diverse viewpoints as possible."[40] In a free market of ideas, wouldn't the truth win out?

Actually, no. More speech across diverse outlets does *not* balance out disinformation, because if no individual network has to be "fair," this incentivizes news siloes that are devoted to skewed content, which is sometimes all that anyone watches. As we have learned in the last decade, when it comes to factual information (and not just opinion- or editorial-based content), balance *across* media sources is not nearly as effective at preventing disinformation as balance *within* media sources.

Obviously, any reimplementation of the Fairness Doctrine would have to be done carefully.[41] First, remember that the original version applied to over-the-air broadcast on public air-waves; but with so much of today's news content on cable TV, which is paid for by individual subscribers to private corporations, would this even apply? And, even if so, there is always the problem of unintended consequences. If we insist that Fox News allow time for opposing viewpoints, wouldn't this also apply to MSNBC and CNN? And might this not exacerbate the problem of false equivalence? The saving grace here would be to remember that, as it was originally conceived, the Fairness Doctrine was concerned with opinion-based editorial content, not facts. If implemented correctly, we wouldn't have to allow equal time for climate deniers (or election deniers) any more than we would for Flat Earthers every time we had a moon launch. Yet who would get to decide what is fact and what is not?

A second idea might be to revise Section 230 of the Communications Decency Act, which gives immunity to website platforms for any liability damages that may arise from third-party content on their pages. In contrast to book, magazine, and newspaper publishers in the United States—which can be sued if they intentionally provide false information—the big tech companies are exempt. In their defense, Facebook, Twitter, and the like tend to say that they are "news aggregators, not publishers," despite the fact that over 70 percent of Americans today get their news from social media platforms.[42] Perhaps it is time for these companies to admit that they are media empires (or at least publishers) and so should be held responsible for the content they amplify on their platforms, even if it is written by others? Behavioral economists have shown that if you provide nudges and incentives for people to change their individual behavior, they often will. The same might presumably work for companies; if they could get sued for sharing disinformation—as other publishers can—just watch it dry up. As of this writing, the US Supreme Court has agreed to take up precisely this question in *Gonzalez v. Google* during its current term, which should be decided by the time you are reading this.[43]

A third possibility, which the social media companies could implement even without any legal or regulatory incentive, would be to get more aggressive about policing not just false *content* but the *known individuals* who are most active in amplifying it. In a recent interview, Clint Watts—a counterterrorism expert, FBI analyst, and former member of the Joint Terrorism Task Force—recommended that the number one way to fight disinformation was to "focus on the top 1 percent of disinformation peddlers, rather than trying to police all false content. If you know who they are, removing the worst offenders or moderating their ability to deliberately broadcast or publicize false content will create an outsized reduction in public harms. We did this in crime and terrorism and other things. Just focus on those that are putting out the most and most prolifically."[44] Remember the study that identified the "disinformation dozen," who spread most of the anti-vax propaganda on Twitter? Why not just deplatform all of them?[45] Note that election disinformation dropped 73 percent just a week after Twitter and a few other platforms cut off Trump![46] It just makes sense. Taking away the microphone from the top disinformers—as ruthlessly as most social media companies police for pornography, beheadings, and terrorism—might have an enormous effect.

A fourth and final strategy might be to focus more attention not just on the behavior of the big three social media platforms—Facebook, Twitter, and YouTube—but also on the stack of other companies that run the Internet, without which the giant user platforms could not run their businesses. According to Joan Donovan—research director at the Shorenstein Center on Media, Politics and Public Policy at Harvard University, and an expert on disinformation—all the Internet companies sit on top of one another like a layer cake. "Online hate and disinformation spread because an entire ecosystem supports them," she is reported to have said.[47] So why not put more pressure also on these "gatekeepers"—the webhosts, web traffic controllers, content delivery networks, and financial service providers (Amazon Web Services, Apple's App Store, GoDaddy, WordPress, Akamai, PayPal, Venmo, and the like)—without whom the big three platforms would be powerless?

Of course, some would hesitate to do *any* of this because they think that any attempt to regulate what gets said on social media is an intrusion on free speech. This, of course, ignores the fact that the First Amendment protects against *government* censorship of individual speech, not private companies, who can deplatform anyone they like. But such hesitation is also ridiculous because it makes it sound as if—in order not to interfere with free speech—we are required to do everything we can to give an immediate, free, and powerful platform to known liars. As if we not only should allow Ku Klux Klan members to get a permit to have a public rally but must volunteer to help them hand out their leaflets too.

In an article entitled "The First Amendment Is Not a Suicide Pact," Jack Snyder writes:

> Many Americans across the full spectrum of opinion—from the progressive left to libertarians to Trump-supporting conspiracy theorists—talk as if the First Amendment guarantees their right not only to voice their opinions in public, but to have instant, unfiltered, global access to an audience of millions, regardless of how ill-founded, incoherent, and misleading those opinions might be.[48]

But that is a ridiculous view and Snyder exposes precisely why. Refusing to amplify disinformation is not the same thing as censorship. Just as you cannot falsely yell "Fire!" in a crowded theater, there should be reasonable limits on platforming for hate speech, election disinformation, pandemic disinformation, and the like, which is the twenty-first-century equivalent of yelling "Fire!" in a public space. But what about the marketplace for ideas? Isn't a free flow of information how truth rises to the surface? Not really. Consider Wikipedia before it took its platform back from the trolls and wreckers;[49] now that it has better content moderation—and is more reliable—some have even called Wikipedia a model for the internet.[50]

Although it may *sound* cheering and patriotic, it is not necessarily true that the best solution to "bad speech" is "more speech," on the theory that truth would inevitably win out over lies. Recent empirical research has shown that, at least with scientific disinformation, lies are quite salient, and once an audience hears disinformation, a predictable percentage will simply believe it no matter what correcting information might later be offered.[51] Although there are steps one can take to mitigate this effect, we cannot debunk our way out of an infodemic. One doesn't fix a polluted information stream simply by diluting it with truth. You have to remove the source of the pollution.

Yet perhaps the best solution of all doesn't have to involve "censorship" so much as *transparency*. One of the most intriguing ideas to fight the amplification of disinformation on the Internet is to *make social media algorithms available to academic researchers*. In keeping with a recent proposal put forward by cognitive scientist Stephan Lewandowsky, why not let cognitive scientists and others study Facebook's and Twitter's algorithms to give a more independent assessment of their potential for public harm?[52] Personal user information could be shielded. Other safety precautions could be taken. Instead, these algorithms are locked up in the hands of the tech companies themselves, so evidence of public harm comes to light only when there is a whistleblower.[53]

And, absent such scrutiny, what is the incentive for social media companies to implement the simplest suggestion of all—tell the truth? As Clint Watts has recently argued, if the social media algorithms are that good at directing people toward salient information, why not take advantage of this power to promote more truth?[54] Right now, so far as we understand it, the social media algorithms are tweaked to promote "engagement," which has the side effect of giving a strategic advantage to disinformers. But what if they were reprogrammed to lead people toward better, more reliable information that is also available on the same platform?

When you watch an anti-vax video on You-Tube, why is it that the next one (or twenty) recommendations all drag you down the same rabbit hole? Couldn't the algorithm be repurposed so that the next thing you saw was something that pushed you back toward more credible information? Yes, of course this is possible . . . but why would the tech giants go for this? Wouldn't it mess up their business model? But if the alternative is regulation, forced transparency, or perhaps antitrust litigation to break these companies up, perhaps they might prefer a solution that they could implement themselves.

There are a plethora of good practical steps that we could take to remove some of the most dangerous tools from the truth killers' hands.

But if we do nothing? Or, almost as bad, if we leave it up to Congress to catch up to this problem in time to make meaningful change? There was a 2021 Senate hearing entitled "Algorithms and Amplification: How Social Media Platforms' Design Choices Shape Our Discourse and Our Minds," which featured testimony from several disinformation experts who were hair-on-fire worried about the problem of algorithmic disinformation, as compared to Congress's ineptitude and misunderstanding of even the most basic issues surrounding the problem.[55] Although we are now mercifully a long way from Republican Senator Ted Stevens's infamous 2006 description of the Internet as a "series of tubes,"[56] there is still a tremendous lack of understanding of what tech companies do (not to mention the stakes we are up against), on both sides of the political aisle.

Senator Chris Coons, a Democrat and head of the Senate committee that sponsored the hearing, said that "there's nothing inherently wrong" with how Facebook, Twitter, and YouTube use their algorithms for the purpose of user engagement, and made it clear that Congress was not weighing any legislation at this point.[57] Contrast this with the apocalyptic stakes described by the experts who testified at the panel.

In her testimony, Joan Donovan put it this way: "The biggest problem facing our nation is misinformation-at-scale. . . . The cost of doing nothing is democracy's end."[58]

5
THE BELIEVERS

At the far end of the disinformation telescope—past the creators and the amplifiers who push out the sludge that pollutes the Internet and the airwaves—are the "believers": the audience for the propaganda who will either buy it or not.

Depressingly, given the fact that the human brain is wired with well over a hundred known cognitive biases, a shocking number of people believe things that aren't supported by the evidence.[1] Remember the idea that all science deniers follow the same flawed reasoning strategy? Step two was belief in conspiracy theories, which turns out to be a pretty good proxy for measuring denialist beliefs.

According to a widely cited 2014 study by J. Eric Oliver and Thomas J. Wood, 50 percent of Americans believe in at least one conspiracy theory:[2]

Nineteen percent believe that 9/11 was an inside job.

Forty percent believe that the Federal Drug Administration is deliberately withholding a cure for cancer.

Nineteen percent think that the Fed deliberately created the 2008 recession. (Notably, the JFK assassination conspiracy theory had to be excluded from the study because it was so widely held that it alone would have skewed the results—despite the fact that one popular assassination conspiracy is now believed to have come from a Russian disinformation campaign.)[3]

Today, the situation hasn't gotten any better.

Twenty-three percent still either strongly or somewhat believe that 9/11 was an inside job.[4]

Twenty-five percent believe that the coronavirus pandemic was planned.[5]

Fifteen percent believe in QAnon (which holds that the US government, media, and financial worlds "are controlled by a group of Satan-worshipping pedophiles who run a global child sex trafficking operation").[6]

And, of course, let's not forget the 32 percent of Americans who have fallen for Trump's big lie that Joe Biden stole the 2020 presidential election.

Is there any hope of convincing these people?

Talking to believers is in some sense like treating the sick once they have already been infected; it's a salvage operation. Once disinformation has made its way out to a virgin population, it is sometimes too late.

One landmark 2019 study by Philipp Schmid and Cornelia Betsch offers a ray of hope, with the first empirical evidence to show that it *is* possible to convince a statistically significant number of science deniers to give up their mistaken beliefs.[7] One way is through "content rebuttal," where experts take on the false facts presented by deniers, but another equally effective method is through "technique rebuttal," where *anyone* can learn how to challenge the flawed five-step method that lies behind denialist reasoning. Yet this process is time consuming. And it doesn't always work. Even this study found that false information was so virulent that even if you debunked it immediately, there was still a stubborn percentage of the population who would not give it up. Other researchers have had better luck with "prebunking,"[8] which aims to inoculate people with good reasoning strategies before they are exposed to any misinformation or disinformation.[9]

But there is more good news. In my book *How to Talk to a Science Denier*, I explore not just the Schmid and Betsch study but also some other research that suggests that how you approach a denier can be just as important as what you say to them. Face-to-face conversation works best, because that is where trust can be built. If we remain calm and employ the tactics of patience, listening, empathy, and respect, it is sometimes possible to talk people out of their anti-vax or climate denial beliefs, as well as even white supremacy or membership in a cult.[10] In fact, in virtually every account I have ever read of a denier who changed their mind, it always happened in the exact same way— through personal engagement with someone they already trusted or had grown to trust. That is why talking directly to a denier might be worthwhile. But the conversation can't just be about sharing facts. Jonathan Swift probably said it best: "You can't reason someone out of something they didn't reason themselves into in the first place." If a denier's beliefs weren't formed on the basis of facts, what makes you think that cramming facts down their throat is going to undo it? Instead, many beliefs— even empirical ones—are about more than just facts. They're about values. They're about what others in their community believe. Often the most important reason why a denier holds a denialist belief is because of how it makes them *feel*.

It may be frustrating not to be able to get through to someone with facts, but remember that most denialism is actually about *identity*. What a denier believes isn't just what they think, it's who they are. So when you attack their beliefs, you are really in some sense attacking them as a person. Indeed, this is what the disinformers want: us versus them, which explains why disinformation is often so polarizing. The point of propaganda is not just to get you to believe false information, but to feel that those on the "other side" are your enemy. By talking to a denier, you are creating an opportunity not just to share facts but to break down any barriers of distrust.

Might this strategy work too for politically motivated "reality deniers"? How will we know, if we aren't talking to one another anymore? I met Dave and Erin Ninehouser—a husband-and-wife team of former labor union organizers—when they helped me publicize a dinner I was hosting in eastern Pennsylvania to talk with coal miners about climate change. In their own work, the Ninehousers go to Trump rallies, where they film their encounters in trying to have respectful, convincing conversations about why their interlocutors should stop watching Fox News or give up the idea that Hillary Clinton belongs in prison. They then use these films to teach classes through their small nonprofit HearYourselfThink, in which they train others to have more meaningful conversations across the partisan divide.[11] Compared to the conversations I've had with Flat Earthers and other science deniers, these are pretty brave folk; and they've been more successful than I have too. Cast your net a little wider, and you'll run across Daryl Davis, the African American blues musician who has talked two hundred members out of the Ku Klux Klan; Steve Hassan, the former Moonie, who recommends similar techniques to talk people out of cults; and the list goes on. In "street epistemology," "motivational interviewing," and "active listening," the efficacy of these same techniques has been proven time and again.

But here we face the crucial question: are such grassroots tools any match for a coordinated campaign of disinformation? The problem is that even if it worked every time, the "talk to them" solution is not really "scalable." Even if we had an army of people out talking to deniers, there is still the problem that once disinformation is out there, most of the damage is already done. But even if talking directly to

believers is not *all* of the solution to our denialist problem these days, it is at least part of it.
Even if we were successful in shutting down the
disinformers and cutting off the amplification
of their message, what to do about the millions
of folks who have already heard the lies and
succumbed to toxic beliefs? In trying to wipe
out the source of a disease, shouldn't we also
care about those who are already sick?

As the Schmid and Betsch study suggests,
some people can be talked back to reality. Others cannot. But if I could guarantee to get *one
single message* out to *all* of the science and reality deniers I've ever met, it would be this: "You
have been lied to." If the primary target of the
truth killers is reality, their collateral victims are
the believers, who are being duped. Good luck
getting them to believe that. As Mark Twain
is purported to have said, "It is easier to fool

someone than to convince them that they have been fooled."

Still, we must try. And this realization is doubly important for those who wish to talk to reality deniers, because it may cause us to have more empathy for them as victims. For your cousin who spouts off about doing his "own research" into how the CDC allegedly suppressed the data on thimerosal, which would allegedly show that the MMR vaccine causes autism. Or your uncle who believes they found bamboo fibers in the ballots in the Arizona recounts, because he heard it on Hannity. Always remember that deniers weren't born, they were made. And if they've changed their minds once, they can change them again.

It is often said that education is the way out of our post-truth crisis, and this may be part of the solution. Along the way, we might try to show the victims of disinformation just who the truth killers are and how they have been waging a campaign to deceive them. To a group of conspiracy-minded folks, it just might work. But we can't wait for the young to be educated, or the denialists to come around, because it takes too long and there are already too many disinformed people out there. Talking face-to-face with believers who have already fallen for the disinformation campaign of Trumpian propaganda is a credible practice, but it cannot be our only weapon to fight back against the truth killers in their war on reality.

So, other than the steps already recommended to push back against the amplifiers and the believers of disinformation, what additional steps might we take? The most important one is to seek a change in our own attitude about what we are up against.

6
HOW TO WIN THE WAR ON TRUTH

The first step in winning an information war is to admit that we are already in one. Remember that denialism isn't an accident or a mistake. It's epistemic homicide. Those who would kill truth would also take steps to cover up their tracks, and in fact the goal of a carefully orchestrated disinformation campaign is to do both things at once. So, since we now know how this happened and who is responsible for it, what is the best way to fight back?

At the US Military Academy at West Point, there is a special group devoted to information warfare. The US Army Cyber Institute employs the conceptual framework of "threatcasting" to think about long-term risks to the future of US security. The future of war is an important topic not only within academic circles at all of the US military academies, but also for planning the practical steps that must be taken by our military leaders to prepare for national defense. In 2020, the US Army Cyber Institute announced that one of the most virulent threats to US security in coming years would be the problem of disinformation, which they explored in a new training manual entitled *Invisible Force*. Most of the book is a graphic novel (a comic book, to be clear . . . this is not your grandfather's US Army) that lays out various stories and scenarios in which military capability and communication is degraded by enemy disinformation. The goal of the book is to get soldiers to imagine how these problems might play out in real life, but the fictional accounts are leavened with short essays on serious topics such as "Microtargeting" and "Post-Truth."

According to Major Jessica Dawson, author of "Microtargeting as Information Warfare" and a specialist on the link between disinformation and extremism at the US Army Cyber Institute, "The real problem these days isn't just that propaganda exists—like leaflets dropped out of a plane during World War II—but that disinformation can now be tailored to hit a receptive audience. Microtargeted online advertising isn't just for selling sneakers or cosmetics—it can be used to market insurgency or hate."[1]

Since it is devoted to national defense against *foreign* enemies, the Cyber Institute does not and cannot consider scenarios under which disinformation might be created by or amplified through domestic sources, even if that propaganda might have originated overseas. Understanding the sheer volume of propaganda that is pushed out every day by Putin-approved troll farms, one must consider the possibility that any Russian disinformation concerning Western vaccines, social unrest, or even US elections might be targeted to appeal as quickly as possible to partisan media outlets in the United States, so that it can be laundered through a domestic news filter. Once Russian propaganda has been picked up by US media, it is off-limits to US military pushback. But that does not mean the threat of domestic information warfare is not still out there, nor is it any less of a risk to our security. Even if they cannot comment on it directly, doesn't the fact that the US Army is taking the threat of disinformation so seriously suggest that the rest of us might do so too?

In a recent conversation with Clint Watts—the former US Army officer, FBI agent, and counterterrorism consultant, who is now deeply involved in preparing the nation against the threat of information warfare—I asked him if there was anything we might learn from the way that the US military fights an information war. In short, are there things that are known to work that we might be doing, but are not merely for our social, political, or cultural reticence to fully embrace what we are up against? He opined that the US military was not actually that good at fighting an information war, due to its structural limitations—because we live in a free society with a democratic form of government, which does not impede the authoritarian regimes that we are usually up against.[2] This, of course, is a virtue for our way of life, but it leaves us vulnerable to exploitation by our adversaries and forces us to fight with one hand tied behind our back. That said, Watts listed several basic principles of information warfare that might provide some practical guidance.

First, we need to increase the number of messengers for truth. We simply need more of them. The truth killers may not be many in number, but they have weaponized an army of believers through the amplification of disinformation. Who is out there on the side of truth to counter that on a day-to-day basis?

Second, we should put more focus on matching the messengers for truth to the people we are trying to reach. Why not find influencers who have greater credibility within the community? "Target not only your message, but your messenger," Watts said. An immediate example springs to mind when one thinks about how epidemiologists and public health officials have struggled to try to convince more people to get their COVID-19 vaccines. After stumbling in some of their initial efforts—especially after the vaccine issue was politicized along partisan lines—public health officials still faced the problem of how to get more African Americans (most of whom were *not* on the GOP side of the partisan spectrum)[3]—to overcome any lingering reluctance to take the shots. Some of this was due to legitimate mistrust over historic instances of deception and mistreatment at the hands of the medical community—like the theft of Henrietta Lacks's DNA or the horrendous Tuskegee Study of untreated syphilis in 1932. At the beginning of the COVID-19 vaccine rollout, Black vaccination rates in the United States lagged behind those for whites. What finally worked? Better public messaging and efforts by grassroots activists who came from the communities they were trying to reach. One of the most incredible stories involved four Black women in rural Alabama who went door to door in their small town to try to convince more people to take the COVID-19 vaccine.[4] In San Francisco, another African American woman single-handedly convinced 1,270 people to get their COVID-19 shots.[5] All of this together eventually led to the Black and white COVID-19 vaccination rates pulling even.[6]

A third piece of advice recommended by Watts was to "repeat the truth more often." As noted earlier, one of the most well-known tactics in the propagandist's playbook is the firmly ensconced "repetition effect." Even if something is untrue, the more we hear it the more credible it sounds. Why do you think Trump kept saying that the Mueller investigation was a "hoax" or that his phone call to the Ukrainian president was "perfect"? He wanted the phrase to stick. But if the repetition effect works for falsehood, couldn't it work for truth too?

If such basic lessons are recommended by those who have actual experience in fighting an information war, perhaps we should listen to them. If we are trying to stop the truth killers, it's time to fight back with our best weapons. And an important part of this is finally to admit what we are up against and stop using euphemisms like "misinformation." The disinformation crisis that is enabling the truth killers to do such violence to our society is not a mistake or even a crime. It is an act of war. And it is time we got on a war footing to fight it.

General Mark Milley, chairman of the Joint Chiefs of Staff under both Donald Trump and President Biden, was reportedly shocked by the insurrection on January 6, but not because he didn't see it coming.[7] It has recently come to light what extraordinary steps Milley took to try to prevent Donald Trump from staging a coup after he had lost the 2020 presidential election, calling Trump's lies about voter fraud a "Reichstag moment."[8] Why take things that seriously? Because, as Milley and others recognized, this was a national security risk. Why take it even more seriously now? Because, as historian Timothy Snyder has said, "a failed coup is practice for a successful coup."[9]

A brief passage from a 2020 article in *New York Magazine* sums it up well:

> "I worry that this whole post-election process has been the dress rehearsal," said Harvard political scientist Steven Levitsky, the other co-author of *How Democracies Die*, citing Vladimir Lenin's

quote that the Russian Revolution of 1905 was the "dress rehearsal" for the October Revolution of 1917, which put the Bolsheviks in power. Levitsky noted that not only have Republicans found that "their base won't punish this sort of behavior, they'll likely applaud it." He added, "none of this stuff can be unlearned."[10]

This same warning is echoed—though now updated with frightening specificity—in Barton Gellman's January 2022 cover story in the *Atlantic*, "Trump's Next Coup Has Already Begun."[11] By hollowing out local election machinery, changing state laws, and making sure that all good Republicans in Congress continue to hew to his big lie, Trump is preparing the ground for what comes next. Fascism. Authoritarianism. Autocracy. What did you think this was about?

Just one election? What is the point of killing truth and swapping in your own version of reality unless you want something enormous? Just as the cigarette companies waged a campaign of science denial in pursuit of billions in profit, Trump and the next generation of truth killers have waged a campaign of reality denial in pursuit of their long-term antidemocratic political goals. #StopTheSteal is the pretext for civil war. The first battle was on January 6, 2021. But if all goes according to plan, there may not need to be another . . . and that may be a very bad thing. Now that Kevin McCarthy and his merry band of cutthroats have taken over the US House of Representatives, two things are clear. First, the Democratic dream of passing the John R. Lewis Voting Rights Advancement Act and the Freedom to Vote Act are dead. No one is coming to save us. And second, the attack on American democracy need not occur now from outside the Capitol, for the number of truth killers *in* Congress has now increased.[12]

Recall that scary moment in a horror film when the wiretapper says, "Wait, the call is now coming from *inside* the house." Now that nineteen states have passed voter suppression laws—with some even enacting legislation that allows their Republican-controlled legislatures to overturn the will of the voters—the GOP-controlled House has all the tools they need to install Trump, DeSantis, or anyone else as president, whether he wins the election or not. This time the truth killers won't need their brainwashed army to carry bats and flagpoles. They'll have the law—and a quorum of lawmakers—on their side.

There was much celebrating by Democrats after they did better than expected in the

2022 midterms—and it looked like Trump's influence on the GOP might be beginning to wane—but the truth is that the forces of autocracy gained ground in 2022. Even if Trump is indicted, doesn't get the Republican nomination for president in 2024, or otherwise leaves the picture, Trumpism remains. Remember that of the 291 election deniers who ran for key federal and state offices in the 2022 midterms, most of them won their races. Although the GOP margin of victory was smaller than pollsters predicted, Republicans still retook the House. This means that those who wish to run another attempt at what almost happened on January 6, 2021, are in a better position to be successful next time, even if Trump is not the candidate who benefits from it.

Recall that Nancy Pelosi was Speaker of the House on January 6, 2021. Who will be in that role on January 6, 2025? It might matter. As Gellman writes in his 2022 essay: "Technically, the next attempt to overthrow a national election may not qualify as a coup. It will rely on subversion more than violence, although each will have its place. If the plot succeeds, the ballots cast by American voters will not decide the presidency in 2024. Thousands of votes will be thrown away, or millions, to produce the required effect. The winner will be declared the loser. The loser will be certified president-elect."[13]

Even though Congress has now updated the Electoral Count Act of 1887, the possibility of a January 6 rerun is still out there.[14] It's right in the third paragraph of Article II, Section I of the US Constitution, which makes clear that in the event of a tie or other failure of one candidate to reach a majority in the electoral college—such

as one state having a disputed set of electors—
the choice of president will be thrown to the
US House of Representatives, where there are
no rules about whom they might choose, other
than that the vote will be taken state by state,
with each one having one vote irrespective of
size. This means that the partisan composition
of each state delegation might be determina-
tive. And in the 118th Congress this consists of
25 states with a majority Republican delegation,
23 with a Democratic one, and two that are tied.
It would take 26 votes to choose a president.

Fortunately, there will be another election
before this happens, and it will be the 119th
Congress (sworn in on January 3, 2025) that will
preside on January 6, 2025.[15] Who will be in control of Congress at that point? No one knows,
and we would be foolish to wait and see.

Because there is still time to stop this.

What might ordinary citizens do to fight back? In addition to the general advice already offered—which might be heeded by government, media, and big tech—what are some practical steps that the rest of us can take?

First, confront the liars. This a lesson learned from how to effectively combat science deniers. If you just let the liar have the microphone, things will only get worse and new recruits will come aboard. As we saw in the January 6th Commission's hearings, simply telling the truth can have a powerful effect. The truth can be an effective weapon against disinformation, but it has to be told—loudly and repeatedly—by its allies. Truth too needs amplification. Stop worrying that you will hurt someone's feelings if you challenge their beliefs and tell them the truth. You are actually doing them a favor.

Second, heed history. Autocrats understand the danger of truth tellers. This is why they make such enormous efforts to shut down dissenters, even when they are few in number and would seem to represent a small threat. Look at Russia. Why did Russia crack down so hard on public displays of protest and shut down all independent media outlets at the beginning of its war with Ukraine? Why does China imprison its dissidents and censor its internet? Because they recognize that truth is a threat against the authoritarian lies they would prefer their citizens to believe. Even in a dictatorship, truth is a weapon. History provides many examples to show that autocrats always go after the truth tellers first. By defending truth, you are thwarting their objective to control the narrative.

A third step that ordinary citizens might take to fight back against reality denial is to resist polarization. Even if you are on the virtuous side of facts and truth, fragmentation is dangerous. Remember that the goal of a disinformation campaign is not merely to get you to doubt, but also to distrust anyone on the other side. When you get to a point where you think of the people who disagree with you as your enemy, the autocrat's work is easier. In that environment, facts don't matter. Deniers don't just have a fact deficit; they also have a trust deficit, which cuts them off from getting reliable information because they are not talking to anyone who disagrees with them. As hard as it is, do not merely retreat to your silo and "be right." Reach out to those who disagree with you, who have been misinformed and disinformed.

If at all possible, try to do so with kindness. They do not need another person to hate or distrust.

Fourth, as hard as it is, recognize that in some sense deniers are victims. They have been duped. They are the zombie foot soldiers of the creators of disinformation, who are profiting by their ignorance, while the believer gets nothing. It may be difficult to feel empathy for someone like this—especially when they are insulting or disrespecting you—but you need to recognize that the target of a disinformation campaign is not just the believers but also the disbelievers. They are polarizing *you* too. Trying to make you feel that it isn't worth it to try to talk to someone on their "team." Ask yourself why cults always insist on keeping their members in an information silo and ban interaction with ex-members or even family.

Fifth, tune out the bullshit. As we've seen, even credible media outlets have a preferred narrative of conflict, failure, and chaos. And this can make you feel powerless. Don't give in to the idea that there is nothing you can do. Even better, insist that your favorite media outlets stop feeding the "both sides" beast that got us here. That they stop normalizing the insurrectionists. That they report on the stakes of all this if democracy fails. We need an army of truth tellers out there. Write to your favorite media outlets. Better yet, write to their advertisers and complain about their coverage. It wouldn't take that many emails *from liberals* to get MSNBC to improve its coverage.

Sixth, don't fall for the sop that this can all be solved by "better education" or "critical thinking." That is important, but it takes a while. And it is hard to get someone to think clearly when they are already in the grips of a conspiracy theory. Yes, we need to teach better critical thinking skills to our children, but we can't wait for them to grow up to save us. But there are some fun and easy steps that adults can take right now to build up our own psychological defenses against mis- and disinformation.[16]

Seventh, stop looking for facile solutions to the problem of disinformation. If this were easy, we would have solved it by now. People around us—especially those who worry about censorship and free speech—love to say that the solution to bad information is good information. But that is not true. Good information is a virtue, but it is not sufficient. We must find a way to stop bad information from being amplified. Do you do business with companies that advertise on Facebook? Let them know that you won't patronize them until they take more of a stand on the problem of disinformation. Are you still on Twitter? Instead of leaving, why not push back against their misguided efforts to promote "free speech" by platforming liars?

Eighth, engage in political activism to try to get Congress to regulate social media. In particular, draw policy makers' attention to the importance of transparency in the algorithms that are used by social media companies to decide what news we will see in our news feeds.[17] It doesn't take that many letters or phone calls from dissatisfied constituents to change a politician's mind. While you're at it, encourage them to push harder for voting rights and electoral reform.

Ninth, take solace in the fact that there are many others out there who are also engaged in this battle. You are not alone. There are millions of people who would like to defend truth and democracy but don't know what to do. Reach out to them. Come up with your own ideas. Lend them this book. But don't grow complacent. We have already seen some violence committed by truth killers around the world—in Putin's Russia, for instance, but also in the United States. And it may grow worse. The transition to autocracy—and the fight against it—can sometimes involve bloodshed.[18] At the very least, expect to be trolled or targeted online. Protect yourself and be prepared.

Tenth, continue to learn more about the problem of reality denial and its consequences for democracy. Just after the 2016 presidential election, I read Timothy Snyder's brilliant manifesto *On Tyranny*, which was part of my inspiration to write this book. Another much longer and carefully researched analysis of the roots of contemporary radicalization in US politics can be found in Yochai Benkler, Robert Faris, and Hal Roberts's extraordinary book *Network Propaganda*, which shows how the "right-wing media ecosystem" has come to dominate so much of today's information content—either in sharing it or responding to it—whatever the platform.[19] Read also the work of Masha Gessen. Nina Jankowicz. Laura Millar. Andy Norman. Peter Pomerantsev. Jonathan Rauch. Thomas Rid. Jen Senko. Jason Stanley. These are the authors who saw this coming. These are the authors who can inspire the actions that will save us.

And let's start working on all of this as soon as possible. The 2022 midterms have already put us a step behind; we could have stopped the Republicans from retaking the House, but we did not. But there's another election coming up in 2024. You may feel encouraged that the 2022 midterms "could have been worse," so there's not much to do now. Or that Congress did finally reform the Electoral Count Act. Or that Trump might disappear from politics. And yes, these are all good things. But disinformation is still rampant throughout the US political system and, until it is defeated, we remain a whisper away from authoritarianism. Unfortunately, many of the best solutions to the disinformation and democracy crisis are ones where we need government or large organizations to take the lead, and by the time this book is published that ship may have sailed. So now we must all just grab an oar and row. Remember the spontaneous street protests after Trump was elected? We can do that again. *Before* the 2024 election.

The truth does not die when liars take power; it dies when truth tellers stop defending it. So let's expose and name the truth killers. Reveal their tactics and their financial ties, and wake up as many of their believers as we can. Boycott the social media companies and anyone else who is enabling them to carry out their dirty mission. Complain to your local cable operator. And, as my favorite bumper sticker from the 2020 election states, "Vote in numbers too big to manipulate."

Even if the coming days are dark, never forget the stakes or the number of people on your side. There are warriors for truth even in electoral dictatorships. Protestors who risk jail or even death, who nonetheless stand up for freedom and democracy, which begins with standing up for truth. Alexei Navalny is a Russian opposition leader and anti-corruption activist who was almost certainly poisoned with a nerve agent by Vladimir Putin's spies in 2020. He nearly died, but after three weeks in a coma, he recovered in a German hospital, after which he was deported back to Russia and imprisoned. From prison, Navalny has engaged in continued acts of protest. He went on a hunger strike. When Russia invaded Ukraine in 2022, he used one of his brief court appearances not to defend himself but to criticize Putin's aggression, after which he went back to his cell. Navalny remains alive due to international attention—both from within Russia and outside it—about his plight.

There are more allies of science, truth, and reality than there are those on the other side. There are more people who know the truth about the 2020 election and January 6 than those who pretend otherwise. And even if the number of disinformation creators, amplifiers, and believers seems dauntingly large, remember that we have history on our side.

***

When I was a boy, I remember the joy of reading the *World Book Encyclopedia*. My family didn't have much money—and neither of my parents had gone to college—but we always had books in the house. The thing I loved most about the encyclopedia was that (as my dad always said) they had "everything" in it. My favorite entries were the ones about logic and science, the philosophers and the writers. I remember marveling that these people had fought through so much to defend such obvious things. Why had the Dark Ages lasted nearly seven hundred years? Who were the idiots who resisted the idea that you needed to wash your hands before performing surgery? Why did the Renaissance wait so long to happen, and why was there anyone against it when it did?

My regret, even in childhood, was that I'd been born too late to defend the things I loved: science, philosophy, and the power of reason. For who was attacking those now? Surely I'd been born into the age in which all truth had finally been discovered. And wouldn't it have been easier to be on the right side of things if I'd been born before so many people were enlightened? Now I could only read about the great intellectual battles of the past. When Socrates was martyred. When Galileo was censured. When Giordano Bruno was burned at the stake.

Yet here I am today fighting for the same things I believed in as a boy. Because what I know now that I did not know then is this: the forces arrayed against the discovery of truth and the use of reason do not die, they wait. They are reborn into every age. It is like hammering mercury. They may disappear for a while, but eventually they gather.

We have been born into an age in which science and reason—indeed truth and reality itself—once again need defending. Embrace that. Don't give in to despair. There is something you can do today to fight back against the truth killers.

Now go out and find it.

ACKNOWLEDGMENTS

This is a short book, but my gratitude toward those who helped me to write it is deep. I would like to thank Kiril Avramov, Jessica Dawson, Mark Pomar, and Clint Watts for allowing me to learn from their expertise as I was doing research, as well as Michelle Daniel who provided crucial guidance along the way. Jonathan Rauch did me the honor of reading and commenting on an earlier draft of what eventually became this book, and gave me great advice and moral support as well. Other invaluable comments were provided by James McIntyre and Robyn

Rosenfeld. To my friends and fellow philosophers Jon Haber and Andy Norman, I am grateful for their keen eye, sharp analysis, and good cheer. The staff at the MIT Press, as always, have been a pleasure to work with.

The dedication for this book goes to my high school history teacher Dave Corkran, who taught me to write, to think, and not to be afraid to stand up for what I believe in. I can think of no more inspiring hope for the future than that good teachers everywhere might emulate his example.

It goes without saying that any errors in this book are my responsibility alone and that the final content is not necessarily reflective of the views of any of the people I have named.

NOTES

Chapter 1

1. Hannah Arendt, *The Origins of Totalitarianism* (New York: Meridian Books, 1958), 474.
2. Timothy Snyder, "The American Abyss," *New York Times*, January 9, 2021, https://www.nytimes.com/2021/01/09/magazine/trump-coup.html.

Chapter 2

1. Naomi Oreskes and Erik M. Conway, *Merchants of Doubt: How a Handful of Scientists Obscured the Truth on Issues from Tobacco Smoke to Global Warming* (New York: Bloomsbury, 2010), 18.
2. Shannon Hall, "Exxon Knew about Climate Change Almost 40 Years Ago," *Scientific American*, October 26, 2015, https://www.scientificamerican.com/article/exxon-knew-about-climate-change-almost-40-years-ago/.

Chapter 3

1. https://skepticalscience.com/history-FLICC-5-techni
   ques-science-denial.html.
2. Chris Mooney, "Ted Cruz Keeps Saying That Satellites Don't Show Global Warming. Here's the Problem," *Washington Post*, January 29, 2016, https://www
   .washingtonpost.com/news/energy-environment/wp
   /2016/01/29/ted-cruz-keeps-saying-that-satellites-dont
   -show-warming-heres-the-problem/; Zeke Hausfather,
   "Major Correction to Satellite Data Shows 140% Fast-
   er Warming since 1998," *Carbon Brief*, June 30, 2017,
   https://www.carbonbrief.org/major-correction-to-sat
   ellite-data-shows-140-faster-warming-since-1998/.
3. Alister Doyle, "Evidence for Man-Made Global Warming Hits 'Gold Standard': Scientists," Reuters, February
   25, 2019, https://www.reuters.com/article/us-climate
   change-temperatures/evidence-for-man-made-global
   -warming-hits-gold-standard-scientists-idUSKCN1
   QE1ZU.
4. Glenn Kessler et al., "Trump's False or Misleading
   Claims Total 30,573 over Four Years," *Washington Post*,
   January 24, 2021, https://www.washingtonpost.com
   /politics/2021/01/24/trumps-false-or-misleading-claims
   -total-30573-over-four-years/.
5. Reid Epstein and Rick Corasaniti, "'Stop the Steal'
   Movement Races Forward, Ignoring Arizona Humil-
   iation," *New York Times*, September 24, 2021, https://
   www.nytimes.com/2021/09/24/us/politics/arizona
   -election-audit-analysis.html.
6. Chris Cillizza, "The Most Absurd Conspiracy Theory
   Yet in the Ongoing Arizona Recount," *CNN*, May 7, 2021,

https://www.cnn.com/2021/05/07/politics/arizona-recount-bamboo-state-senate/index.html.

7. Li Cohen, "6 Conspiracy Theories about the 2020 Election Debunked," *CBS News*, January 15, 2021, https://www.cbsnews.com/news/presidential-election-2020-conspiracy-theories-debunked/.

8. Yevgeny Kuklychev, "January 6 Conspiracy Theories and False Narratives One Year On," *Newsweek*, January 6, 2021, https://www.newsweek.com/january-6-conspiracy-theories-false-narratives-one-year-1666212.

9. Michael Wines, "Cyber Ninjas, Derided for Arizona Vote Review, Says It Is Shutting Down," *New York Times*, January 7, 2022, https://www.nytimes.com/2022/01/07/us/cyber-ninjas-arizona-vote-review.html.

10. Tovia Smith, "Why Is the 'Big Lie' Proving So Hard to Dispel?" *NPR*, January 4, 2022, https://www.npr.org/2022/01/04/1070337968/why-is-the-big-lie-proving-so-hard-to-dispel.

11. Brian Naylor, "Read Trump's Jan. 6 Speech, A Key Part of Impeachment Trial," *NPR*, February 10, 2021, https://www.npr.org/2021/02/10/966396848/read-trumps-jan-6-speech-a-key-part-of-impeachment-trial.

12. Solomon Asch, "Opinions and Social Pressure," *Scientific American* 193, no. 5 (November 1955): 31–35, https://pdodds.w3.uvm.edu/teaching/courses/2009-08UVM-300/docs/others/everything/asch1955a.pdf; Juliet Macur, "Why Do Fans Excuse the Patriots' Cheating Past?" *New York Times*, February 5, 2017, https://www.nytimes.com/2017/02/05/sports/football/new-england-patriots-super-bowl-cheating.html.

13. Hugo Mercier and Daniel Sperber, "Why Do Humans Reasons? Arguments for an Argumentative Theory,"

Behavioral and Brain Science 34, no. 2 (April 2011): 57–74, https://pubmed.ncbi.nlm.nih.gov/21447233/.

14. Caitlin Dickson, "Poll: Two-Thirds of Republicans Still Think the 2020 Election Was Rigged," *Yahoo News*, August 4, 2021, https://news.yahoo.com/poll-two-thirds-of-republicans-still-think-the-2020-election-was-rigged-165934695.html.

15. Robert Post, "The Other Tragedy of January 6," *Atlantic*, January 16, 2021, https://www.theatlantic.com/ideas/archive/2021/01/the-other-tragedy-of-january-6/617695/.

16. Jonathan Rauch, "How to Beat Trump and Co. in Their War on Truth: Lessons from the Arizona 2020 Election 'Audit,'" *New York Daily News*, May 22, 2021, https://www.nydailynews.com/opinion/ny-oped-arizona-dreaming-20210522-uyd6ivuv75hd5gof2geyd5adtu-story.html.

17. Lee McIntyre and Jonathan Rauch, "A War on Truth Is Raging. Not Everyone Realizes We're in It," *Washington Post*, June 25, 2021, https://www.washingtonpost.com/opinions/2021/06/25/war-truth-is-raging-not-everyone-recognizes-were-it/.

18. Rob Kuznia et al., "Stop the Steal's Massive Disinformation Campaign Connected to Roger Stone," *CNN*, November 14, 2020, https://www.cnn.com/2020/11/13/business/stop-the-steal-disinformation-campaign-invs/index.html.

19. Brian Stelter, "This Infamous Steve Bannon Quote Is Key to Understanding America's Crazy Politics," CNN.com, November 16, 2021, https://www.cnn.com/2021/11/16/media/steve-bannon-reliable-sources.

20. Christopher Paul and Miriam Matthews, "The Russian 'Firehose of Falsehood' Propaganda Model," Santa Monica: Rand Corporation, 2016, https://www.rand.org/pubs/perspectives/PE198.html.

21. Jobby Warrick and Anton Troianovski, "Agents of Doubt," *Washington Post*, December 10, 2018, https://www.washingtonpost.com/graphics/2018/world/national-security/russian-propaganda-skripal-salisbury/?utm_term=.0a3322c4d2f3&itid=lk_interstitial_manual_103.

22. Jonathan Rauch, "Trump's Firehose of Falsehood," *Persuasion*, November 18, 2020, https://www.persuasion.community/p/trumps-firehose-of-falsehood.

23. Matthew Luxmoore, "Putin's Performance at Geneva Summit Seen as a Master Class in 'Whataboutism,'" *Radio Free Europe*, June 17, 2021, https://www.rferl.org/a/putin-biden-summit-whataboutism-russia-narrative/31313209.html.

24. Personal communication with Avramov on November 15, 2021.

25. Sean Illing, "The Russian Roots of Our Misinformation Problem," *Vox*, October 26, 2020, https://www.vox.com/world/2019/10/24/20908223/trump-russia-fake-news-propaganda-peter-pomerantsev.

26. Danielle Kurtzleben, "Trump Embraces One of Russia's Favorite Propaganda Tactics—Whataboutism," *NPR*, March 17, 2017, https://www.npr.org/2017/03/17/520435073/trump-embraces-one-of-russias-favorite-propaganda-tactics-whataboutism.

27. William J. Broad, "Putin's Long War against American Science," *New York Times*, April 13, 2020, https://www

.nytimes.com/2020/04/13/science/putin-russia-disin
formation-health-coronavirus.html.

28. William J. Broad, "Putin's Long War Against American
Science," *New York Times*, April 13, 2020, https://www
.nytimes.com/2020/04/13/science/putin-russia-disin
formation-health-coronavirus.html.

29. Henry Miller, "Russia's Anti-Vaccine Propaganda Is
Tantamount to a Declaration of War," *PRI Center for
Medical Economics and Innovation*, March 29, 2021,
https://medecon.org/russias-anti-vaccine-propaganda
-is-tantamount-to-a-declaration-of-war/.

30. Michael R. Gordon and Dustin Volz, "Russian Disinformation Campaign Aims to Undermine Confidence
in Pfizer, Other COVID-19 Vaccines, U.S. Officials Say,"
Wall Street Journal, March 7, 2021, https://www.wsj
.com/articles/russian-disinformation-campaign-aims
-to-undermine-confidence-in-pfizer-other-covid-19
-vaccines-u-s-officials-say-11615129200; Simon Lewis,
"U.S. Says Russian-Backed Outlets Spread COVID-19
Vaccine 'Disinformation,'" Reuters, March 7, 2021,
https://www.reuters.com/article/us-usa-russia-covid
-disinformation/u-s-says-russian-backed-outlets
-spread-covid-19-vaccine-disinformation-idUSKBN2B
0016.

31. Leonid Savin, "Bill Gates, Vaccinations, Microchips,
and Patent 060606," *Oriental Review*, April 29, 2020,
https://orientalreview.org/2020/04/29/bill-gates-vacci
nations-microchips-and-patent-060606/comment
-page-1/.

32. "Poll: 44% of Republicans Think Bill Gates to Use
COVID-19 Vaccine to Implant Tracking Chip," *CBS*

Austin, May 26, 2020, https://cbsaustin.com/news/local/poll-44-of-republicans-think-bill-gates-to-use-covid-19-vaccine-to-implant-tracking-chip.

33. Jamie Dettmer, "Russian Anti-Vaccine Disinformation Campaign Backfires," *Voice of America*, November 18, 2021, https://www.voanews.com/a/russian-anti-vaccine-disinformation-campaign-backfires/6318536.html.

34. Rauch, "How to Beat Trump and Co." *New York Daily News*, https://www.nydailynews.com/opinion/ny-oped-arizona-dreaming-20210522-uyd6ivuv75hd5gof2geyd5adtu-story.html.

35. Peter Wehner, "You're Being Manipulated," *Atlantic*, July 9, 2021, https://www.theatlantic.com/ideas/archive/2021/07/jonathan-rauch-americas-competing-totalistic-ideologies/619386/.

36. Jonathan Rauch, "Arizona's Election Audit Is an Attack by Americans on Other Americans," *Arizona Central*, June 13, 2021, https://www.azcentral.com/story/opinion/op-ed/2021/06/13/trump-using-arizona-election-audit-russian-style-disinformation-campaign/7585784002/.

37. James Davitt Rooney, "Trump Is Biggest Presidential Loser since Hoover," *Commonwealth*, November 17, 2020, https://commonwealthmagazine.org/opinion/trump-is-biggest-presidential-loser-since-hoover/.

38. Fredreka Schouten, "19 States Passed This Year Laws to Restrict Voting, New Tally Finds," *CNN*, October 4, 2021, https://www.cnn.com/2021/10/04/politics/voting-laws-restrictive-map-october/index.html.

39. Amy Gardner, "All but Two McCarthy Defectors in House Are Election Deniers," *Washington Post*,

January 3, 2023, https://www.washingtonpost.com/na
tion/2023/01/03/mccarthy-defectors-election-deniers/.

40. Fiona Hill, "The Kremlin's Strange Victory," *Foreign
Affairs*, September 29, 2021, https://www.foreignaf
fairs.com/articles/united-states/2021-09-27/kremlins
-strange-victory.

Chapter 4

1. Shannon Bond, "Just 12 People Are Behind Most Vaccine Hoaxes on Social Media, Research Shows," *NPR*,
May 14, 2021, https://www.npr.org/2021/05/13/996570855
/disinformation-dozen-test-facebooks-twitters-ability
-to-curb-vaccine-hoaxes.

2. Elizabeth Dwoskin, "Massive Facebook Study on Users' Doubt in Vaccines Finds a Small Group Appears
to Play a Big Role in Pushing the Skepticism," *Washington Post*, March 14, 2021, https://www.washington
post.com/technology/2021/03/14/facebook-vaccine
-hesistancy-qanon/.

3. Jonathan Mahler and Jim Rutenberg, "How Murdoch's Empire of Influence Remade the World," *New
York Times*, April 3, 2019, https://www.nytimes.com
/interactive/2019/04/03/magazine/rupert-murdoch-fox
-news-trump.html.

4. "A Rigorous Scientific Look into the 'Fox News Effect,'" *Forbes*, July 21, 2016, https://www.forbes.com
/sites/quora/2016/07/21/a-rigorous-scientific-look-into
-the-fox-news-effect/?sh=647b05fe12ab.

5. Mark Jurkowitz et al., "U.S. Media Polarization and
the 2020 Election: A Nation Divided," *Pew Research*

Center, January 24, 2020, https://www.pewresearch.org
/journalism/2020/01/24/u-s-media-polarization-and
-the-2020-election-a-nation-divided/.

6. Brian Stelter, *Hoax: Donald Trump, Fox News, and the
   Dangerous Distortion of Truth* (New York: Simon &
   Schuster, 2021), 151.

7. Pamela Engel, "The US Intelligence Report on Russian Hacking Directly Implicates WikiLeaks," *Business
   Insider*, January 6, 2017, https://www.businessinsider
   .com/us-intelligence-report-wikileaks-russian-hacking
   -2017-1.

8. Peter Suciu, "Tucker Carlson Accused of Promoting Russian Propaganda as Putin Masses Forces on
   Ukraine Border," *Forbes*, December 8, 2021, https://
   www.forbes.com/sites/petersuciu/2021/12/08/tucker
   -carlson-accused-of-promoting-russian-propaganda
   -as-putin-builds-up-forces-on-ukraine-border/?sh
   =7f6510538ef3.

9. Julia Davis, "Kremlin TV Worries Tucker Carlson's
   Pro-Putin Bias Has Gone Too Far," *Daily Beast*, January 26, 2022, https://www.thedailybeast.com/tucker
   -carlsons-pro-putin-bias-has-gone-too-far-kremlin-tv
   -says.

10. Rosalind Helderman, Emma Brown, Tom Hamburger,
    and Josh Dawsey, "Inside the 'Shadow Reality World'
    Promoting the Lie That the Presidential Election Was
    Stolen," *Washington Post*, June 24, 2021, https://www
    .washingtonpost.com/politics/2021/06/24/inside-shadow
    -reality-world-promoting-lie-that-presidential-elec
    tion-was-stolen/; Anna Massoglia, "Details of the
    Money behind Jan. 6 Protests Continue to Emerge,"

Open Secrets, October 25, 2021, https://www.opensecrets
.org/news/2021/10/details-of-the-money-behind-jan-6
-protests-continue-to-emerge/; Beth Reinhard, Jacque-
line Alemany, and Josh Dawsey, "Low-Profile Heiress
Who 'Played a Strong Role' in Financing Jan. 6 Rally
Is Thrust into Spotlight," *Washington Post*, December
8, 2021, https://www.washingtonpost.com/investiga
tions/publix-heiress-capitol-insurrection-fancelli/2021
/12/08/5144fe1c-5219-11ec-8ad5-b5c50c1fb4d9_story
.html; Igor Derysh, "How One Billionaire Family
Bankrolled Election Lies, White Nationalism—at the
Capitol Riot," *Salon*, February 4, 2021, https://www
.salon.com/2021/02/04/how-one-billionaire-family
-bankrolled-election-lies-white-nationalism--and-the
-capitol-riot/.

11. Jane Mayer, "The Big Money behind the Big Lie," *New
Yorker*, August 9, 2021, https://www.newyorker.com
/magazine/2021/08/09/the-big-money-behind-the-big
-lie.

12. Jennifer Rubin, "Forget Partisan Scorekeeping. Our
Ukraine Policy Isn't about Instant Results," *Washington
Post*, February 27, 2022, https://www.washingtonpost
.com/opinions/2022/02/27/media-narrative-ukraine/.

13. "Broken Media—Official Documentary," https://www
.youtube.com/watch?v=XOOxMAkLuoU.

14. Steve Hoffsteter (@SteveHoffsteter), "'If someone says
it's raining and another person says it's dry, it's not
your job to quote them both. Your job is to look out
of the fucking window and find out which is true.'
Sheffield University Journalism lecturer Jonathan
Foster," Twitter, December 3, 2020, 2:59 p.m., https://

twitter.com/stevehofstetter/status/13345881112175165
45?lang=en.

15. "'Don't Book Liars': Soledad O'Brien Challenges Media at Disinformation House Hearings," *USA Today*, February 25, 2021, https://www.usatoday.com/videos /entertainment/tv/2021/02/25/soledad-obrien-chal lenges-media-house-hearing-disinformation/681347 5002/; Marcia Apperson, "Consider Using a 'Truth Sandwich' to Counter Misinformation," *PBS*, April 22, 2020, https://www.pbs.org/standards/blogs/standards -articles/what-is-a-truth-sandwich/; Maxwell Boykoff and Jules Boykoff, "Balance as Bias: Global Warming and the US Prestige Press," *Global Environmental Change* 14 (2004): 125–136, https://www.eci.ox.ac.uk /publications/downloads/boykoff04-gec.pdf.

16. One exception here has been Nicolle Wallace's show *Deadline: White House* on MSNBC, which has been quite good about telling the disinformation story.

17. Masha Gessen, *Surviving Autocracy* (New York: Riverhead, 2020), 151.

18. Julia Ioffe (@juliaioffe), "I repeat: the only people who were fully prepared to cover the Trump presidency properly were people who knew how authoritarian regimes worked. The Washington press corps, which treats politics as something between a baseball game and a Broadway show, was woefully unprepared," May 20, 2022, 12:05 a.m., https://twitter.com/juliaioffe/status /1527500693283684366?lang=en.

19. "House Hearing on Disinformation and Extremism in Media," *C-SPAN*, February 24, 2021, https://www.c -span.org/video/?509245-1/house-hearing-disinforma tion-extremism-media.

20. Perry Bacon Jr., "How Media Coverage Drove Biden's Political Plunge," *Washington Post*, July 17, 2022, https://www.washingtonpost.com/opinions/2022/07/17/media-bias-role-biden-approval-decline/.

21. Christine Chan and Lisa Shumaker, "U.S. Records over 25,000 Coronavirus Deaths in July," Reuters, July 31, 2020, https://www.reuters.com/article/us-health-coronavirus-usa-july/u-s-records-over-25000-coronavirus-deaths-in-july-idUSKCN24W1G1.

22. Kelsey Vlamis, "Fox News and Tucker Carlson Use 'Minute by Minute' Ratings That Show Their Audience Love 'White Nationalism' Talking Points, Report Says," *Yahoo News*, April 30, 2022, https://news.yahoo.com/fox-news-tucker-carlson-minute-014055697.html; "How Newsrooms Blame the Audience—The Problem with Jon Stewart—Apple TV+," https://www.youtube.com/watch?v=Bl17xMFiEFw.

23. Davey Alba, "YouTube's Stronger Election Misinformation Policies Had a Spillover Effect on Twitter and Facebook, Researchers Say," *New York Times*, October 14, 2021, https://www.nytimes.com/2021/10/14/technology/distortions-youtube-policies.html.

24. Geoffrey Fowler, "Twitter and Facebook Warning Labels Aren't Enough to Save Democracy," *Washington Post*, November 9, 2020, https://www.washingtonpost.com/technology/2020/11/09/facebook-twitter-election-misinformation-labels/.

25. Damian Carrington, "'A Great Deception': Oil Giants Taken to Task over 'Greenwash' Ads," *Guardian*, April 19, 2021, https://www.theguardian.com/business/2021

/apr/19/a-great-deception-oil-giants-taken-to-task
-over-greenwash-ads.

26. Alexis Madrigal, "This Is How Much Fact-Checking Is
Worth to Facebook," *Atlantic*, February 1, 2019, https://
www.theatlantic.com/technology/archive/2019/02
/how-much-factchecking-worth-facebook/581899/.

27. Spencer Ackerman, "Facebook Now Says Russian Dis-
info Reached 150 Million Americans," *Daily Beast*, November 1, 2017, https://www.thedailybeast.com/face
book-now-says-russian-disinfo-reached-150-million
-americans.

28. "Facebook Says Took Down 1.3 Billion Fake Accounts
in Oct–Dec," Reuters, March 22, 2021, https://www
.reuters.com/technology/facebook-disables-13-billion
-fake-accounts-oct-dec-last-year-2021-03-22/; "Mark
Zuckerberg Says Facebook Has Removed 8 Million
Posts with COVID Misinformation, but Won't Say
How Many People Viewed Them," *CBS News*, August
18, 2021, https://www.cbsnews.com/news/mark-zucker
berg-facebook-covid-misinformation-post/.

29. Adi Robertson, "Facebook Says It's Spent $13 Billion on
'Safety and Security' since 2016," *The Verge*, September
21, 2021, https://www.theverge.com/2021/9/21/22685863
/facebook-safety-security-staff-spending-misinforma
tion-abuse-wall-street-journal-reports.

30. Adrian Chen, "The Laborers Who Keep Dick Pics and
Beheadings Out of Your Facebook Feed," *Wired*, October 23, 2014, https://www.wired.com/2014/10/content
-moderation/.

31. "The Facebook Files," *Wall Street Journal*, https://www
.wsj.com/articles/the-facebook-files-11631713039.

32. Sheera Frenkel and Cecilia Kang, *An Ugly Truth: Inside Facebook's Battle for Domination* (New York: Harper, 2021).

33. Kevin Roose, "Facebook Reverses Postelection Algorithm Changes That Boosted News from Authoritative Sources," *New York Times*, December 16, 2020, https://www.nytimes.com/2020/12/16/technology/facebook-reverses-postelection-algorithm-changes-that-boosted-news-from-authoritative-sources.html.

34. Nitish Pahwa, "The Facebook Crisis in India Might Be the Worst Facebook Crisis of All," *Slate*, October 26, 2021, https://slate.com/technology/2021/10/facebook-papers-india-modi-misinformation-rss-bjp.html; Dan Milmo, "Rohingya Sue Facebook for 150bn over Myanmar Genocide," *Guardian*, December 6, 2021, https://www.theguardian.com/technology/2021/dec/06/rohingya-sue-facebook-myanmar-genocide-us-uk-legal-action-social-media-violence.

35. Michelle Toh, "Facebook Sued for $150 Billion over Violence against Rohingya in Myanmar," *CNN*, December 7, 2021, https://www.cnn.com/2021/12/07/tech/facebook-myanmar-rohingya-muslims-intl-hnk/index.html.

36. Mathew Ingram, "What Should We Do about the Algorithmic Amplification of Disinformation?" *Columbia Journalism Review*, March 11, 2021, https://www.cjr.org/the_media_today/what-should-we-do-about-the-algorithmic-amplification-of-disinformation.php.

37. Isobel Asher Hamilton, "Mark Zuckerberg says Whistleblower's Claims That Facebook Places Profit over People 'Don't Make Any Sense,'" *Business Insider*,

October 6, 2021, https://www.businessinsider.com/mark-zuckerberg-facebook-whistleblower-claims-dont-make-sense-2021-10./

38. Sophie Zhang, "Don't Blame Russian Trolls for America's Anti-vaxx Problem. Our Misinformation Is Homegrown," *Guardian*, August 18, 2021, https://www.theguardian.com/technology/2021/aug/18/facebook-fazze-russian-trolls-anti-vaxx-misinformation.

39. Sarah Olutola, "Nicki Minaj's COVID-19 Vaccine Tweet about Swollen Testicles Signals the Dangers of Celebrity Misinformation and Fandom," *The Conversation*, September 20, 2021, https://theconversation.com/nicki-minajs-covid-19-vaccine-tweet-about-swollen-testicles-signals-the-dangers-of-celebrity-misinformation-and-fandom-168242; Geoff Brumfiel, "The Life Cycle of a COVID-19 Vaccine Lie," *NPR*, July 20, 2021, https://www.npr.org/sections/health-shots/2021/07/20/1016912079/the-life-cycle-of-a-covid-19-vaccine-lie.

40. Terry Francke, "Expand Fairness Doctrine beyond Airwaves?" Calaware.org, December 16, 2008, https://calaware.org/fairness-doctrine-expanded-beyond-airwaves/.

41. Victor Pickard, "The Fairness Doctrine Won't Solve Our Problems—But It Can Foster Needed Debate," *Washington Post*, February 4, 2021, https://www.washingtonpost.com/outlook/2021/02/04/fairness-doctrine-wont-solve-our-problems-it-can-foster-needed-debate/.

42. Andrew Hutchinson, "New Research Shows That 71% of Americans Now Get News Content via Social Platforms," *Social Media Today*, January 12, 2021, https://

www.socialmediatoday.com/news/new-research-shows-that-71-of-americans-now-get-news-content-via-social-pl/593255/.

43. Ian Millhiser, "A new Supreme Court Case Could Fundamentally Change the Internet," *Vox*, October 6, 2022, https://www.vox.com/policy-and-politics/2022/10/6/23389028/supreme-court-section-230-google-gonzalez-youtube-twitter-facebook-harry-styles.

44. Personal communication with Clint Watts on May 28, 2022.

45. Steven Salzberg, "De-platform the Disinformation Dozen," *Forbes*, July 19, 2021, https://www.forbes.com/sites/stevensalzberg/2021/07/19/de-platform-the-disinformation-dozen/?sh=4e3d61af7378. As of November 2022, only 4 of the 12 seem to have been deplatformed and 8 of the 12 still had active accounts on Twitter.

46. Elizabeth Dwoskin and Craig Timberg, "Disinformation Dropped Dramatically the Week after Twitter Banned Trump and Some Allies," *Washington Post*, January 16, 2021, https://www.washingtonpost.com/technology/2021/01/16/misinformation-trump-twitter/.

47. Geoffrey Fowler and Chris Alcantara, "Gatekeepers: These Tech Firms Control What's Online," *Washington Post*, March 24, 2021, https://www.washingtonpost.com/technology/2021/03/24/online-moderation-tech-stack/.

48. Jack Snyder, "The First Amendment Is Not a Suicide Pact," *American Purpose*, May 5, 2021, https://www.americanpurpose.com/articles/the-first-amendment-is-not-a-suicide-pact/.

49. The watershed year was 2006: Katie Hafner, "Growing Wikipedia Refines Its 'Anyone Can Edit' Policy,"

New York Times, June 17, 2006, https://www.nytimes
.com/2006/06/17/technology/17wiki.html.

50. Benjamin Klutsey, "Defending the Constitution of Knowledge," *Discourse*, June 25, 2021, https://www.discoursemagazine.com/ideas/2021/06/25/defending-the-constitution-of-knowledge/.

51. Philipp Schmid and Cornelia Betsch, "Effective Strategies for Rebutting Science Denialism in Public Discussions," *Nature* 3 (2019): 931–939, https://www.nature.com/articles/s41562-019-0632-4.

52. Stephan Lewandowsky, "Combatting Knowledge Dementors," *Pontifical Academy of Social Sciences*, The Vatican, September 14, 2021, http://www.pass.va/content/dam/scienzesociali/booklet/booklet_post_truth.pdf, https://www.youtube.com/watch?v=jZHrb-72rrg.

53. Ben Smith, "A Former Facebook Executive Pushes to Open Social Media's 'Black Boxes,'" *New York Times*, January 2, 2022, https://www.nytimes.com/2022/01/02/business/media/crowdtangle-facebook-brandon-silverman.html.

54. Personal communication with Clint Watts, December 8, 2021.

55. https://www.judiciary.senate.gov/meetings/algorithms-and-amplification-how-social-media-platforms-design-choices-shape-our-discourse-and-our-minds.

56. Ken Belson, "Senator's Slip of the Tongue Keeps on Truckin' over the Web," *New York Times*, July 17, 2006, https://www.nytimes.com/2006/07/17/business/media/17stevens.html.

57. Makena Kelly, "Congress Is Way behind on Algorithmic Misinformation," *The Verge*, April 27, 2021, https://

www.theverge.com/2021/4/27/22406054/facebook-twit
ter-google-youtube-algorithm-transparency-regula
tion-misinformation-disinformation.

58. Statement of Joan Donovan to the Senate Committee
on the Judiciary Subcommittee on Privacy, Technology, and the Law, April 27, 2021, https://www.judiciary
.senate.gov/imo/media/doc/Donovan%20Testimony
%20(updated).pdf.

Chapter 5

1. Ben Yagoda, "Your Lying Mind," *Atlantic*, September
2018, https://www.theatlantic.com/magazine/archive
/2018/09/cognitive-bias/565775/.

2. J. Eric Oliver and Thomas J. Wood, "Conspiracy Theories and the Paranoid Style(s) of Mass Opinion,"
American Journal of Political Science 58, no. 4 (October
2014): 952–966, https://onlinelibrary.wiley.com/doi/abs
/10.1111/ajps.12084; John Sides, "Fifty Percent of Americans Believe in Some Conspiracy Theory. Here's
Why," *Washington Post*, February 19, 2015, https://www
.washingtonpost.com/news/monkey-cage/wp/2015
/02/19/fifty-percent-of-americans-believe-in-some
-conspiracy-theory-heres-why/.

3. Tim Weiner, "This Is Where Oliver Stone Got His Loo-
ny JFK Conspiracies From," *Rolling Stone*, November
22, 2021, https://www.rollingstone.com/politics/poli
tics-features/jfk-oliver-stone-conspiracy-theory-russian
-disinformation-1260223/.

4. Statista Research Department, "Belief That September
11 Was an Inside Job in the Unisted States in 2019," June

14, 2022, https://www.statista.com/statistics/959504/belief-september-11-inside-job-conspiracy-us/.

5. Katherine Schaeffer, "A Look at the Americans Who Believe There Is Some Truth to the Conspiracy That COVID-19 Was Planned," *Pew Research Center*, July 24, 2020, https://www.pewresearch.org/fact-tank/2020/07/24/a-look-at-the-americans-who-believe-there-is-some-truth-to-the-conspiracy-theory-that-covid-19-was-planned/.

6. Chuck Todd et al., "Study Finds Nearly One-in-Five Americans Believe QAnon Conspiracy Theories," *NBC News*, May 27, 2021, https://www.nbcnews.com/politics/meet-the-press/study-finds-nearly-one-five-americans-believe-qanon-conspiracy-theories-n1268722.

7. Philipp Schmid and Cornelia Betsch, "Effective Strategies for Rebutting Science Denialism in Public Discussions," *Nature Human Behavior* 3 (2019): 931–939, https://www.nature.com/articles/s41562-019-0632-4.

8. Sander Van Der Linden et al., "Inoculating against Misinformation," *Science* 358, no. 6367 (December 1, 2017): 1141–1142, https://www.science.org/doi/10.1126/science.aar4533.

9. https://cognitiveimmunology.net/about-circe.

10. Lena Sun and Maureen O'Hagan, "'It Will Take Off Like Wildfire': The Unique Dangers of the Washington State Measles Outbreak," *Washington Post*, February 6, 2019, https://www.washingtonpost.com/national/health-science/it-will-take-off-like-a-wildfire-the-unique-dangers-of-the-washington-state-measles-outbreak/2019/02/06/cfd5088a-28fa-11e9-b011-d8500644dc98_story.html; Jason Samenow, "NASA Head Jim Bridenstine, Once Doubtful, Confirms He Believes Humans

Are the Leading Cause of Climate Change," *Washington Post*, May 23, 2018, https://www.washingtonpost.com/news/capital-weather-gang/wp/2018/05/23/nasa-head-jim-bridenstine-once-doubtful-confirms-he-believes-humans-are-the-leading-cause-of-climate-change/; Dwane Brown, "How One Man Convinced 200 Ku Klux Klan Members to Give Up Their Robes," *NPR*, August 20, 2017, https://www.npr.org/2017/08/20/544861933/how-one-man-convinced-200-ku-klux-klan-members-to-give-up-their-robes; Rachael Allen, "The Man Who Wants to Free Trump Supporters from 'Mind-Control,'" *Slate*, June 1, 2021, https://slate.com/human-interest/2021/06/steven-hassan-former-moonie-trumpism-cult-theory.html.

11. https://hearyourselfthink.org/.

Chapter 6

1. Personal communication with Jessica Dawson, June 6, 2022; Jessica Dawson, "Microtargeting as Information Warfare," *Cyber Defense Review* (Winter 2021): 63–79, https://cyberdefensereview.army.mil/Portals/6/Documents/2021_winter_cdr/04_CDR_V6N1_Dawson.pdf.
2. Personal communication with Clint Watts, December 8, 2021.
3. Gaby Galvin, "Racial Gaps in Vaccine Willingness Are Narrowing, but Partisan Ones Persist," *Morning Consult*, March 17, 2021, https://morningconsult.com/2021/03/17/covid-vaccine-partisan-racial-gaps-poll/.
4. Mia Jankowicz, "How 4 Black Alabama Women Went Door-to-Door Persuading People to Get Jabbed in One

of the Least Vaccinated US States," *Business Insider*, September 29, 2021, https://www.businessinsider.com/what-its-like-to-go-door-door-promoting-vaccine-alabama-2021-9.

5. Michelle Robertson, "This SF Woman Convinced 1,270 People to Get Vaccinated. Here's Her Secret," *SF-GATE*, August 12, 2021, https://www.sfgate.com/bayarea/article/felisia-thibodeaux-vaccination-it-bookman-inglesid-16382590.php.

6. Audra Burch and Amy Schoenfeld Walker, "Why Many Black Americans Changed Their Minds about COVID Shots," *New York Times*, October 16, 2021, https://www.nytimes.com/2021/10/13/us/black-americans-vaccine-tuskegee.html.

7. Susan Glasser, "What Does National Security Even Mean Anymore, after January 6th and the Pandemic?" *New Yorker*, March 4, 2021, https://www.newyorker.com/news/letter-from-bidens-washington/what-does-national-security-even-mean-anymore-after-january-6th-and-the-pandemic.

8. Kevin Breuninger, "Top U.S. Gen. Mark Milley Feared Trump Would Attempt a Coup after His Loss to Biden, New Book Says," *CNBC*, July 15, 2021, https://www.cnbc.com/2021/07/15/mark-milley-feared-coup-after-trump-lost-to-biden-book.html.

9. Dana Milbank, "This Historian Predicted Jan 6. Now He Warns of Greater Violence," *Washington Post*, July 15, 2021, https://www.washingtonpost.com/opinions/2021/07/15/american-democracy-survived-its-reichstag-fire-jan-6-threat-has-not-subsided/.

10. Ben Jacobs, "Is Trump's Coup a 'Dress Rehearsal'?" *New York Magazine*, December 27, 2020, https://nymag

   .com/intelligencer/2020/12/historians-fear-trumps-failed
   -coup-is-a-dress-rehearsal.html.

11. Barton Gellman, "Trump's Next Coup Has Already Begun," *Atlantic*, December 6, 2021, https://www.the atlantic.com/magazine/archive/2022/01/january-6-in surrection-trump-coup-2024-election/620843/.

12. Adrian Blanco, Daniel Wolfe, and Amy Gardner, "Tracking Which 2020 Election Deniers Are Winning, Losing in the Midterms," *Washington Post*, November 7, 2022, https://www.washingtonpost.com/politics /interactive/2022/election-deniers-midterms/?itid=lk _inline_manual_31.

13. Barton Gellman, "Trump's Next Coup Has Already Begun," *Atlantic*, December 6, 2021, https://www.the atlantic.com/magazine/archive/2022/01/january-6-in surrection-trump-coup-2024-election/620843/.

14. Kyle Cheney, "Efforts to Trump-Proof Presidential Certification Crash into Congressional Realities," *Politico*, January 1, 2022, https://www.politico.com/ news/2022/01/01/congress-future-presidential-ballots -trump-challenge-526168.

15. Elaine Kamarck, "What HAPPENS if Trump and Biden TIE in the Electoral College?" *Brookings* (blog), October 21, 2020, https://www.brookings.edu/blog /fixgov/2020/10/21/what-happens-if-trump-and-biden-tie -in-the-electoral-college/.

16. Jon Roozenbeek, Sander van der Linden, and Thomas Nygren, "Prebunking Interventions Based on 'Inoculation' Theory Can Reduce Susceptibility to Misinformation across Cultures," *Misinformation Review*, February 3, 2020, https://misinforeview.hks.harvard.edu /article/global-vaccination-badnews/.

17. Stephan Lewandowsky and Anastasia Kozyreva, "Algorithms, Lies, and Social Media," *NiemanLab*, April 7, 2022, https://www.niemanlab.org/2022/04/algorithms-lies-and-social-media/.
18. Barbara F. Walter, "'These Are Conditions Ripe for Political Violence': How Close Is the US to Civil War?" *Guardian*, November 6, 2022, https://www.theguardian.com/us-news/2022/nov/06/how-close-is-the-us-to-civil-war-barbara-f-walter-stephen-march-christopher-parker.
19. Timothy Snyder, *On Tyranny: Twenty Lessons from the Twentieth Century* (New York: Tim Duggan Books, 2017); Yochai Benkler, Robert Faris, and Hal Roberts, *Network Propaganda: Manipulation, Disinformation, and Radicalization in American Politics* (New York: Oxford University Press, 2018).

INDEX